D1518329

Coping WITH

Confrontations

and Encounters

with the Police

Claudine G. Wirths, M.A., M.Ed.,
Mary Bowman-Kruhm, Ed.D.

Confrontations

and Encounters

with the Police

**Claudine G. Wirths, M.A., M.Ed.,
Mary Bowman-Kruhm, Ed.D.**

THE ROSEN PUBLISHING GROUP, INC./NEW YORK

Published in 1998 by The Rosen Publishing Group, Inc.
29 East 21st Street, New York, NY 10010

Cover Photo by Christine Innamorato

First Edition

Library of Congress Cataloging-in-Publication Data
Wirths, Claudine G.
    Coping with confrontations and encounters with the police /
Claudine G. Wirths, Mary Bowman-Kruhm.
        p.   cm.
    Includes index.
    Summary: A practical guide to minimize risks when dealing with
police officers and law enforcement procedures.
    ISBN 0-8239-2431-9
    1. Police—United States—Juvenile literature.   2. Police
questioning—United States—Juvenile literature.   3. Arrest—United
States—Juvenile literature.   4. Public relations—Police—United
States—Juvenile literature.   [1. Police.   2. Arrest.]   I. Bowman-
Kruhm, Mary.   II. Title.
HV7922.W553   1998
363.2'0973—dc21   97-19059
                                                                 CIP
                                                                  AC

Manufactured in the United States of America.

For
all the men and women
who keep the peace
● ● ●

Thanks to:

Michael Boyd, Faculty, Frederick (MD) Community College; Wade Collins, Student, Frederick, MD; Joan Lumley, Teacher, Montgomery County (MD) Public Schools; Eva Shackelford, Social Worker, Montgomery County (MD) Public Schools; Truman and Sherri Theofield, Martinsburg, PA.

With special thanks to:

Dr. Hiawatha B. Fountain, Montgomery County (MD) Public Schools; E. M. Hanna, Greenville, SC; Jeff Levine, Psychology Student and Police Aide, Auxiliary Division, University of Maryland; Dr. James Nickell, Faculty, St. Mary's College, St. Mary's, MD; Darryl Norwood, Montgomery County (MD) Public Schools/ Court Liaison; Wesley Pomeroy, Retired Director, Task Force, Miami, FL; Major R. R. Raffensberger, Chief of Police, Frederick, MD; Margo Reiser, Coordinator, Office of Reading, Craighead County Jonesboro (AR) Public Library; Major Richard K. Williams, Chief of Police, Madison, WI.

About the Authors

Claudine G. Wirths, M.A., M.Ed., and **Mary Bowman-Kruhm**, Ed.D., have coauthored twenty books. *I Hate School: How to Hang In & When to Drop Out* (Harper & Row, 1987) was named by the American Library Association on its lists "Best Books for Young Adults—1986" and "Recommended Books for Reluctant Young Adult Readers—1987."

Other books include *Where's My Other Sock? How to Get Organized & Drive Your Parents & Teachers Crazy* (Harper, 1989); *I Need a Job* (J. Weston Walch, 1988); *Are You My Type? Or Why Aren't You More Like Me?* (Consulting Psychologists Press, 1992); *How to Get Up When Schoolwork Gets You Down* (David C. Cook, 1993); *Word Power*, *Your Circle of Friends*, and *Your New School* in the "Time to Be a Teen" series for Henry Holt/21st Century Books (1993); *Choosing Is Confusing: How to Make Good Choices, Not Bad Guesses* (CPP/Davies-Black Publishing, 1994); *Upgrade: The High Tech Road to School Success* (CPP/Davies-Black Publishing, 1995); and *I Need to Get Along with Other People* (Walch, 1995).

In addition, Wirths and Bowman-Kruhm are the authors of numerous articles and stories in professional journals and magazines such as *Guide Magazine*, the *Learning Disabilities Association Advocate*, and *Vegetarian Times*. They are contributing editors to *Children's Book Insider* newsletter. Together and separately, they make presentations to groups of students, teachers, and parents on a variety of topics.

Contents

CHAPTER 1

You and the Police

You hear the siren before you see the flashing lights in the rearview mirror.

"That can't be for me," you think. "I haven't done anything wrong."

You drive on. Soon the police car is close to your back bumper, lights blazing, siren whining.

"I think that cop wants you to pull over," your passenger says.

"Can't mean me," you reply.

Are you saying to yourself, "I stay out of trouble. I don't need to know how to get along with the police"? If you think that way, we say to you, "Good luck!"

We can think of two major reasons why you need to know how to cope with the police:

- First, chances are that something, even if it's accidental, will happen in your life that involves you with the police.
- Second, the huge number of people involved in law-enforcement work and their presence in everyday public life makes avoiding the police unlikely.

Something Will Happen to You

Trying to stay out of trouble helps and is the right thing to do, but it is no guarantee that you can avoid the police. Maybe you'll be in a car accident and the police will want to know what happened. Maybe the crowd at a concert will turn mean and riot. Maybe you'll simply be in the wrong place at the wrong time—or maybe you'll get caught breaking a law.

With the increase in crime in many areas, you may also need police help. Maybe someone will break into your home, and you'll report the theft of your television set. Maybe your street will become a hangout for drug dealers. Maybe you will be mugged.

Sooner or later, guilty or innocent, you will find yourself involved with the police.

Police Are Everywhere

The second major reason why you need to get along with police officers is because there are so many of them. If you're like most people, when you think of the police you think primarily of local police and state highway patrols. Depending on where you live, you may include sheriffs and their deputies in the kinds of police you know.

In reality, however, there are dozens of kinds of police. Park rangers and marine patrols are also considered police, as are federal police like the Drug Enforcement Agency (DEA), the Immigration and Naturalization Service (INS), the Border Patrol, the U.S. Marshal Service, the Secret Service, the Customs Service, the Coast Guard, and many others. In fact, there are more than 40,000 police agencies and more than half a million persons employed in them.

Some communities also have volunteer police, auxiliary police, and reserve police. In addition to police hired by the local, state, and federal governments, there are also thousands of people who are hired privately, such as mall guards or security guards, who perform police-like services.

As we said, sooner or later you will encounter the police.

Knowing How to Cope Is Essential

In today's world, knowing how to cope effectively with the police is not just sensible—it's essential. What you say and how you behave when you interact with the police can have a big impact on your life. If the police charge that you're guilty of a major crime, like manslaughter, your behavior can affect the rest of your life. If you are guilty of a minor offense, like speeding or disorderly conduct, your actions might make the difference between a fine and a jail sentence. If you're not guilty of any crime, the wrong actions can pave the way for a lot of unnecessary hassle. Even if you simply want the police to help you, you may not get their full support if you don't treat them with respect.

Did the Officer Want You?

At the beginning of the chapter we left you driving with a friend, sure you hadn't done anything wrong, not knowing whether you should pull the car over. You finally decide that the cop means you, so you stop the car on the side of the highway and look in the rearview mirror. You see the officer get out of his car and walk quickly up to your driver's-side window, his hand resting on his gun.

Which of these things are likely to happen to you when you realize that you are about to be confronted and questioned by the police officer?

- Your palms begin to sweat and your heart beats faster.
- You take a deep breath, but it doesn't really seem deep enough.
- You feel nervous and fearful.

Having all of those reactions in a tense situation is natural to all of us. Primitive people had to be ready to deal with fierce animals, so their bodies were prepared for instant "fight or flight" when faced with sudden danger. Few of us today face these same dangers, but our bodies are still programmed for either a fight or flight at times of high stress. For most of us, a confrontation with the police is perceived as one of those situations, no matter how innocent we believe ourselves to be.

Can you stop how your body reacts at that moment? No. Your body responds naturally. Your brain can't stop your body from having those automatic reactions, but it can prevent you from acting on them. Because we live in a civilized society, fighting or running are no longer our only choices.

Controlling your responses, however, is easier said than done when you're face to face with a problem. Since the growing tensions in our society mean that sooner or later you will encounter the police, now is the time to look at options for controlling your responses to a confrontation.

This book will help you think about those other options. We will talk about various ways to respond when you are stopped, questioned, accused, or arrested by the police.

To help you cope with the police, we will:

- give you tips for coping in any encounter, major or minor;
- show you how your actions and words can give you some control over what happens;
- tell you how to get maximum help from the police;
- describe some ways for you to minimize becoming a victim of crime;
- give you resources for further reading; and
- provide a glossary of words commonly used in connection with police encounters and arrests.

At the very least, we hope to save you from making a serious mistake when an officer confronts you or you need an officer's help. You may even find that what you read in this book can someday save your life.

Face to Face

You invite a few good friends to spend Saturday evening at your place. At a little past 11 PM, the amps are roaring out some great music and there are loads of chips and drinks. Everything is going the way you like it. Suddenly you hear a loud knock at the door. You open it, and there stands a police officer.

The young officer says in a gruff voice, "What's going on here? We had a call from your neighbors that this party is getting too loud."

What would you say?

- "So what? We're not causing any trouble!"
- "Who cares what those f—ers next door say! Go catch some real criminals instead of busting on us."

- "We'll turn down the sound. Thanks for the warning."
- "Come on in! There's always room for one more."

Your answer probably reflects your personal feelings about the police. Here are the kinds of experiences that may have contributed to the way you feel about the police:

- What you've heard your parents, family members, and friends say.
- Police officers you have seen in action.
- What you've learned about police at school.
- Dealings you or your family have had with the police.
- Books you've read, movies you've seen, and television shows you've watched.
- Any officers you have known personally.
- The attitude you have toward anyone in authority.

Why You Can Envy, Fear, Like, and Hate Police— All at the Same Time

Police stand for many different things—power, help, support, danger, excitement, and even fear. Because of this, most of us have mixed feelings about them. If we are talking about an individual officer, we may like that person. If we are talking about police in general, we may remember how we were helped when we were in a car accident. Or we may think about how they broke down the door of our apartment, looking for drugs. If we're late and drive too fast, we hope we'll avoid seeing any police. If we are about to be mugged, we hope a whole squad of officers will suddenly appear.

These mixed feelings are mostly based on the different messages about police that we have received from childhood. We were told that if we were lost, we should tell a policeman. But we were also told not to talk to strangers, and yet the police are usually strangers. Some of us were told that if we were bad the police would come and get us, and yet we met "Officer Friendly" in first grade. We may have been told that the police in our town hate people like us, but we may have been proud of a parent on the force. No wonder we all have such mixed feelings!

In this book, we will not try to change your personal feelings about law enforcement officers. We will, however, try to help you sort out your feelings about police and understand them. First, it will help to know more about the work of the police.

What Do the Police Do?

Where do you get your information about the work police officers do?

- "I have a cousin who's a cop. He tells me lots of great stories."
- "I watch lots of television shows. I see how the police work."
- "In my town they don't do much. We might as well call 7-11 instead of 9-1-1 if we need help."

You may feel that you already know what police do, but you are probably basing your impressions on the police work you see on television, the police you see on the streets and highways of your town, or officers you may know. Your perceptions are likely to be limited or even inaccurate.

In most television shows, viewers see police chasing and catching criminals in thirty minutes flat—two hours, if the show is a special. Police work actually takes a lot longer, and crimes are seldom solved so quickly or cleanly. Gunfire and car chases are rare, and few officers look as great as the ones on the screen. The police on television often break laws in solving cases, such as firing into crowds of people or stealing evidence. These shows may be fun to watch, but they present a lot of misleading information.

In contrast to what you see on television, police and their departments vary a great deal from one place to another. A four-person police force in a small midwestern town has little in common with the huge Los Angeles force, except in the overall nature of their duties.

In a small town, the police officers know, or may even be related to, many of the people they assist or arrest. A resident of a small town, known personally by an officer, may be treated in an informal way, even if suspected of committing a crime.

Large city police departments tend to be more impersonal toward the people they serve because they rarely know them. In a large city, suspects are more likely to be handled according to the letter of the law, regardless of who they are.

However large or small a department is, the basic policing functions are the same. The police are there to uphold the laws, keep the peace, and protect the citizens.

Linda has been a police officer on a small police force in a midwestern farming community for two years. "I thought the job would be exciting more of the time," she says. "Exciting things do happen now and then, but most of the time I walk around and ticket illegally parked cars and talk about drug abuse to the kids at school. At night I ride through lover's lane a few times and check buildings to be sure they are properly locked. You wouldn't think police work could get boring, but it does. Most of the so-called crimes that happen in our town are committed by teenagers who break into a neighbor's house because they have nothing better to do.

"Sometimes we sit around the station and wish something big would happen. But then when something big does happen, three or four other things always seem to happen at the same time. Then there aren't enough of us to go around. Phones ring off the hook, and all of us work around the clock.

"When the crisis is over, we feel great if we have caught the criminal and put him behind bars. On those days I don't want to be anything but a police officer."

The truth is that police on patrol do spend much of their time on routine jobs like directing traffic, patrolling streets and roads, and checking store alarms at night. But there is also a saying among patrol officers that their jobs are "hours and hours of boredom broken by moments of pure panic."

Do you want a job in which you may have to:

- pull a dead child from a car wreck?
- persuade a man not to shoot himself or others he is holding hostage?
- talk to a woman who has been raped?
- tell parents that their son is a drug dealer?
- walk into a dark alley alone when you know an armed robber is hiding there?

None of these responsibilities sound pleasant or easy, do they? But they are part of every officer's job. Police work is a high-stress career. Officers have to be ready to deal with murder victims, suicides, horrible accidents, natural disasters, and other such situations. They are also under strain because often their numbers are too few for the demands made on them. They rush from call to call and can give only short attention to the less dangerous crimes or citizen complaints.

Because of their job demands, officers sometimes are not as friendly as we would like. The violence and cruelty and tragedy that most officers face also cause some of them to act in an impersonal manner to help them handle the strain of the job.

On the television program "Meet the Press" on April 14, 1996, Janet Reno, speaking as Attorney General of the United States, said, "Law enforcement is one of the toughest jobs in America today."

Because they are the police, we take for granted that the men and women in law-enforcement jobs will do whatever needs to be done to *enforce the law*, *keep the peace*, *and protect us*. Those three phrases sum up the work of the police.

The Police as Community Parents

In a way the police are like community "parents." We tend to take what they do for granted, just as we might with our own parents. Most of us expect our family to come to our aid when we have a problem. In the same way, we expect the police to help us when we face difficult situations. We expect them to keep our traffic flowing, protect us and our homes, be at the scene of traffic accidents, arrest criminals, and stop domestic disputes. We also expect them to find lost children, give us directions, wait patiently while we gather change for the parking meter, and be "Officer Friendly" when kids approach.

Officer Hiers walked the streets of a small North Carolina town. One day on routine patrol, he noticed a small boy in a parked car. At the same time, the little boy saw Officer Hiers and began knocking on the car window. Hiers looked around and, seeing no one, went over to the child.

"Mr. Policeman," the little boy said. "Can you take me to the bathroom? My mother said if I was ever in trouble I should tell a policeman. And I am about to be in big trouble."

Officer Hiers tried not to laugh. Instead he asked where the boy's mother was. Learning that she had gone into the nearby bank, Hiers promised the little boy that he would get help quickly. He brought the embarrassed mother back to the car, and the little boy beamed his thanks.

When the boy grew up, Officer Hiers never ceased to tease him about the incident. It made the two friends for life.

You may be surprised to learn that some citizens take the work of police so much for granted that they make all kinds of crazy requests of them. A group of police officers once talked about strange things they had been asked to do. One said he had been asked to help push a car stuck in mud. Another was enlisted to catch a runaway racehorse. But the winner was an officer who said he had been asked to open a pickle jar by a woman who didn't have anyone around the house to help her. While opening pickle jars is not in the job description, this officer had handled her request with a smile, as the police often do.

Who Wants to Be a Police Officer?

Police come from all walks of life. Salaries generally make a career in law enforcement a good job for an ambitious young person who likes the work and the life. Most departments now work actively to hire women and minorities to the force. But there are still traces—more in some departments, less in others—of unfair hiring and unfair advancement.

The ordinary police officer today is an educated, physically-fit man or woman of any race. Most of them have families, go to church or temple or mosque, have hobbies, enjoy an evening out or a day off, want to do a good job, and carry out the day-to-day tasks of their jobs with grace and skill. These men and women believe the work they do for all of us is important, and they wear their badges proudly.

My name is Rick. I wanted to be a policeman from the time I was a little boy. I hung around my uncle a lot. He was a policeman, and when he was off duty he took me hunting with him and told me all kinds of great stories about his work. Then, when I was about fourteen, he was killed trying to stop a bank robber. From that time on, I made up my mind to become a police officer.

Toward the end of high school, I joined the police intern program. As soon as I turned twenty-one, I took all the tests and was accepted to the police academy.

Well, I have been an officer for twenty years. I have never gotten that guy that killed my uncle, but I have nailed lots of other criminals, and I think my uncle would be proud of me. Police work has been good for me. All of my friends are cops and we take care of each other in good times and bad. I can't imagine doing anything else.

Police work appeals strongly to men and women who come from police families. Those who have served in the military also join the ranks of law enforcement in large numbers. Some people seek police jobs because they want to help and protect others. There are also people who apply for police jobs because they have been victims of a crime and want revenge. Some are adventure seekers. A few like the idea of the authority and power over other people that they gain by doing police work.

Do We Need Police?

If you had to make a change in the way the law is enforced, would you:

- get rid of all the police and let people handle crime on their own?
- hire more police so there would be plenty around when we need them?
- train the police better?

Before you answer, think what life in the United States would be like if we had no police. Your first thought may be that "no police" sounds like a great idea—you could drive as fast as you like, take anything you want, knock down anyone who got in your way. But think further.

Nothing you own and no one you love or care about would be safe. The smallest action, like crossing a street, or driving a car, or going to the mall, would be filled with danger. The weak, the ill, the very young, and the very old would be helpless to protect themselves. In truth, we would all be at the mercy of the biggest bullies who had the biggest guns. Believe it or not, back in the 1600s that's how it was in our country.

Let's look at the power that the police have to protect us, our families, and the things we own, and how that power has grown so that some people now question it.

CHAPTER 2

The Power of the Police

W hat would you say if someone asked how you feel about the power of the police?

- "They have way too much power. They act like bullies."
- "I think they have just about the right amount of power."
- "I don't think they have enough power. If they had more power, there would be a lot less crime."

How the Police Came to Have Power

In the early days of the United States, the military protected citizens from Native American and pirate raids, and fought wars with other countries; but people soon realized that they needed protection from others who broke the law. Soon towns were hiring local police, called constables as they were in England, to keep law and order.

As people moved into the undeveloped West, the guns and knives they needed to survive and protect themselves with were also being used to settle everyday disputes. To cope with the lawless frontier, the job of the sheriff evolved. If a sheriff needed help, he called on able-bodied citizens and formed them into a "posse." Posse comes from the Latin term *posse comitatus*, meaning "the power of the county." U.S. and local marshals also carried out court orders and other law-enforcement jobs.

But by the mid-1850s, much of the country was lawless. Because people wanted their property and the safety of their families protected from those who broke the law, citizens saw the need for strong local law enforcement. Cities and towns began to establish police departments with the power to protect the people, preserve the peace, and enforce the laws.

As you can see, when the United States was still a very young country, law-enforcement officers were given the power to protect citizens. From our earliest history, our leaders did not believe that just any citizen should be allowed to take personal action to deal with crime. No one, no matter how rich or powerful, would have the right to catch criminals unless that person was hired as a law-enforcement officer.

Police power comes from all of the people. By choosing to live in this country, you, as a citizen, agree that the police will represent you when a crime is committed. For example, if someone steals your car, you do not have to look for the thief. The police do it for you. The principle behind this system is that no matter how weak or powerless you are, if a crime is committed against you the full power of your government will step in to protect you.

That is why the killing of a police officer is such a serious matter. The death of a police officer is like losing someone in our own family. We each lose the personal power of protection that officer represented.

They're Not Like Family to Me

"Wait a minute!" you may be saying. "I don't think of the police as family. Not in my neighborhood. They let the big crooks go and arrest people who are just trying to make a living. If we call for help, it may be hours before they come, if they come at all. I wouldn't even trust one to help me with my grocery bags."

You are not alone in thinking that way. No doubt about it—the power of the police is a fact of life, and many people question that power. But is the problem with the amount of power the police have, or with misuse of that power? Let's look at the question a little further.

> The older officer held the long-haired teenager against the van. The teen's wrists were cuffed behind his back.
>
> "Hey, look at this," the younger officer called over as he reached under the front seat. He flipped the lid off a small black plastic container. Inside was white powder, not the roll of 35 mm film it had once held.
>
> "It's cocaine all right," he said.
>
> "You dirty punk!" the first officer screamed into the young man's face. "It's scum like you who sold that poison to my son."
>
> He whirled the teenager around and hit him in the nose with his fist. The young man fell to the ground. The other officer ran over and kicked the suspect in the ribs. A blow from the first officer's nightstick broke the young man's arm.

Then the two officers dragged the screaming, bleeding youth into the squad car and took him to the station. The officers' written report, later used in court, read that the suspect had "violently resisted arrest."

Such incidents are not common, despite what you may have seen or read. Most of the police you meet will treat you fairly and respect your rights. But a small percentage won't, and you can't tell from looking at an officer whether he or she will treat your fairly. You need to understand more about police power and what that power, misused or not, means to you.

Misuse of Power

The problem of police's misuse of power goes back to the first police departments. The first police units were made up mostly of white males who had no special training or education but were willing to take on the low-paying job of keeping law and order. In truth, political bosses often controlled who were hired and how they carried out their jobs.

As time passed, people became aware of the difference between good and bad police work. A few large city departments began training programs. Still, corruption and misuse of power existed in many departments.

After World War II, towns and cities often hired returning soldiers as police officers. Some of these men had received police training in the military, but few towns and cities funded programs to teach officers how to carry out the job of policing in the community.

By the 1950s, a typical small town probably had a force made up of ten or fifteen white men. The chief of police and his men did not have to pass any tests to be hired. They didn't even have to be able to read and write very well. Once hired, each man was given a uniform, a badge, a nightstick, handcuffs, and a pistol. Then he was sent out on the street to work. Training took place on the job.

These officers knew little or nothing about the laws. They enforced the laws the chief told them to enforce. Since they often had received their jobs as a personal or political favor, they were free to mistreat minorities and to use the law to the advantage of the rich and powerful, who had helped to place them in the job.

Despite unfair hiring practices and poor training, many policemen did outstanding jobs. Then, as now, officers lost their lives in gunfights with criminals. Others were injured trying to rescue people from burning cars. They worked night and day if a child was lost or kidnapped. In times of crisis, they almost all met the challenge.

The year was 1958.

"I really feel sorry for Jake's wife," said Detective Grant to the other men on the Aiken, South Carolina, police force. "She's a good woman—helps out at church all the time—but when I went to their house to arrest Jake for shooting deer out of season again, she told me the kids were going to go hungry if I confiscated the deer. I had to take the deer, but I sure hate to see them without food. Look, I'm going to throw some money in my hat and then pass the hat around. Put in what you can, and I'll take it out to her tonight along with a sack of groceries. Okay?"

The officers all tossed in money out of their own pockets. Grant went back to Jake's place that night, not only with money but also with bread and soup and cakes contributed by several of the officer's wives.

Stories like the above usually went unnoticed by the average, middle-class, white citizen. In fact, many people knew little of what the police did, good or bad. They saw the police only as community helpers they could call upon if needed. On the other hand, most people were also unaware of the prejudiced, brutal, and even criminal acts sometimes committed by the men hired to protect their town.

The 1960s Bring Change

By the 1960s, three changes were taking place in the United States that would affect police work:

- Television, with on-the-spot reports of news events, had become common.
- The civil rights movement was gaining strength.
- Many young people experimented with a wide variety of drugs and they also began protesting the Vietnam War.

Around the end of the 1960s all of these events came together to change police work. Before that time, few people had confrontations with police because most misbehavior by young people was handled at home or at school. Families had little or nothing to do with the police.

But in the 1960s, the evening television newscasts began to educate the majority of the country. What people saw made a huge impact on their feelings about the police. In many cases, police brutality shocked viewers. Night after night, they saw that those who had little money or status and who lived in poor neighborhoods or slums were rarely protected by the police. If they were accused of a crime, guilty or not, these people were often mistreated.

Viewers saw dogs and fire hoses turned on African Americans when they tried, lawfully, to integrate schools. They also saw Hispanics and Native Americans beaten by impatient police.

But the real shock came to white, middle-class Americans when some of their own sons and daughters participated in Vietnam protests. Some protesters openly smoked marijuana. The police tried to enforce the law and control the crowds. The young people fought back and called the police "pigs." Police hit them with nightsticks and sprayed tear gas. College students who never in their lives expected to be arrested found themselves locked up in bug-infested jails. Their parents were stunned as, day after day, they watched the news of these protests on television, or had to go to the station house to bail out their child, now marked with an arrest record for the rest of his or her life.

Clearly, the nation had to take the problem of police work and the use of police power more seriously. The best police administrators in the country worked with citizen leaders to propose drastic changes in training and hiring practices. These reforms were generally backed by local political leaders, who allotted money for training and better salaries. These changes came slowly, however, because we have a civil police system and reform had to take place one department at a time, all across the nation.

A Civil Police System

The United States has what is called a civil police system. Civil means that citizens have a say through their power to vote in what laws are established and how laws are enforced. The country is not policed by a single agency. Police power is divided into literally thousands of separate agencies spread across cities, towns, counties, states, and the federal government.

Our government uses a military policing system only in times of serious public crisis, such as a disastrous earthquake or a major riot. The President of the United States or the governor of a state can declare "martial law" and can send the army or National Guard to the area. The local police must then answer to the military. As soon as the crisis is over, the area reverts to the control of the local police.

Most police agencies do operate to some degree as military units. The officers wear uniforms and use ranks to show official grades or positions in that unit. These outward signs do not mean, however, that we have a national or a military police.

Using—and Misusing—Power

Since the beginning of our police system in the mid-1800s, our country has grown both in size and population, and its laws have become more complex. Likewise, the work of policing has grown. To carry out the huge job now entrusted to them, the police must have a great deal of power.

When individual police officers misuse their power, however, they create a serious problem. Communities have learned that they must select the right people for the job and train them to use their power wisely. Good police departments try to screen out men and women who are hungry for power or are otherwise unfit for this challenging job.

How Police Learn Their Job

Almost every police department in this country requires new recruits to have at least a high-school education. More and more departments require a college degree for advancement. More of them are likely to do so in the future.

In the average department, the rookie officer undergoes several weeks of training. He or she also attends refresher training programs during the course of his or her career.

The basic training courses teach the officers a variety of subjects including:

- The laws they are to uphold
- The laws governing police behavior
- Ways to collect evidence
- Conduct when making arrests
- Police-community relations
- The use of firearms
- Physical fitness
- Procedures in dangerous and emergency situations

After passing basic training, most officers are on probation for a year. During that year they go on patrol with a seasoned officer and learn the street side of police work. This trial period is a large part of an officer's training. The year with a skilled officer gives a rookie the experience and know-how to do the job.

Many people may seem like good choices for police work and do well at the academy. Once on the street, however, they may find they can't stand the strain of the actual job and quit.

All of these training experiences help shape how an officer uses his or her power. Other factors can also influence an officer's use of power to carry out duties:

- Laws differ from one community to another.
- Communities expect the police to practice selective law enforcement.

Why Law Enforcement Varies

Communities differ widely in local laws and the way those laws are enforced. Local laws are passed by the citizens of each town, county, or state, based on what they believe is important. Citizens of one town may forbid walking on the grass in the park. Citizens of another town may not consider that a problem.

The enforcement of the same law also depends heavily on concerns of the local citizens. For example, the seat of a county where most people make their living growing tobacco may not be likely to enforce state law on the sale of cigarettes to minors. But another town may be strict in enforcing this law.

Selective law enforcement is inevitable, even though police are charged with enforcing all laws. A department selects which laws to enforce because:

- it lacks the resources to arrest and try every person who breaks a law;
- the wording of some laws is unclear;
- the officers would have to break other laws to enforce one law, for example, they have to speed to catch someone who is speeding;
- arrests would not solve the problem, for example, if an elderly senile person shoplifts, the problem is

better handled by referral to the person's family, not by arrest;
- many laws are out of date.

Many laws stay on the books long after the reason for them has been forgotten. Here are a few:

- An elephant cannot be used to plow a field in North Carolina.
- Eating rattlesnake meat on Sunday is against the law in Kansas.
- In Vermont, a law forbids building a fence that allows sheep to escape.

How Do You Know Which Laws Will Be Enforced?

In each community, the importance of certain laws is taken for granted by the people who live there.

If you want to know what people think is important, read the local paper. Listen to the people waiting in line for a movie, or at the grocery store. The more people talk about a problem, the more likely the police will enter the picture. If everyone is talking about the number of accidents at the corner of Jay Street and Main, look out; your chances of getting a ticket for coasting through the stop sign at that intersection are high.

If you move to a new town or county, check with other people your age to find out which laws the police are sure to enforce. For example:

- An adult may be able to buy alcohol legally in town but not in the dry county only a few miles away.
- Buying lottery tickets may be okay, but betting on sports may be illegal.

- Driving an all-terrain vehicle (ATV) on the beach may be allowed, but only in certain specified areas.

Sometimes the laws that are strictly enforced change within a town. Such a change often follows a serious crime or accident that upsets many people. You might see on television that the mayor's son is caught in a drug bust. Suddenly more people start worrying about kids and drugs. They ask the police to enforce a local law about selling cigarette papers to minors. If you work in a store that sells papers to teens, this news should tip you off to stop selling to them.

The power of the public and the local press are the primary forces that influence the makeup of the police and the direction of police work. If the police in your city or town are not enforcing the laws that most people support, citizens can unite through their clubs, churches, schools, and civic groups to insist on better hiring and training practices and proper police conduct. They can do this through the media and by voting for public officials who share these goals.

In the long run, however, the laws that are enforced and the use of power in enforcing those laws depend primarily on the officer who responds to the call.

When the Police Get a Call

For the police, the word "call" has at least two meanings in connection with the enforcement of laws.

- First, there is the actual call, or request for action.
- Second, there is the judgment call of how to handle the situation. Police must use their own judgment about whether to make an arrest or handle the

problem in some other way. This is the time when officers choose how much or how little power to use in carrying out their duty.

On the scene of a call, an officer usually tries to choose the response that will best handle the situation. The officer may or may not always follow the letter of the law. Choosing the best response, however, is often difficult. The officer must make decisions quickly and the choice may have long-term effects, not only on those at the scene but on the officer as well.

For example, suppose Officer Jane D. receives a call that a fight has broken out among three men at the corner of South and Sixth Streets. When the officer arrives on the scene, she must use her judgment on how much power to use in response. Her decision is based on her knowledge of the law, the persons involved, and common sense.

She must consider what she knows about fights here and how local residents expect one to be handled. Each community has its own view of what police are expected to do in certain situations. She must consider whether the men have had prior trouble with the law and how dangerous they are to one another, to her, and to innocent bystanders. She must consider what impact her actions will have on the bystanders. Will they report to friends that the police handled the situation well? Or will they convey bad feelings that will hinder police work in the future? Should she handle the situation alone or call for backup? All of these considerations must be taken into account by an officer responding to a call.

Even a law governing a serious crime is not always the sole basis for the officer's call about how to handle a situation. For example, tampering with mail is a major federal crime. So anyone caught fooling around with mail that isn't theirs should be arrested, right? But consider the following two instances of tampering with mail. If you were the police officer in each situation, what would you say and do if you apprehended the teenager?

- Someone reports that a teenager you know to be mentally challenged is opening mailboxes and looking at the letters; the young man lives in the neighborhood. He sometimes gets into minor mischief, but he is not really a troublemaker.
- Someone reports that a teenager is taking mail from several mailboxes and looking at the letters. No one has seen him in the neighborhood before.

In situations like those, most officers want to use as little power as is needed. They are trained to respond in that way. The law actually tells police how much force they can use in given situations.

Because officers choose to use very little power in most situations, many young people fail to realize the enormous power that all police officers have.

Police Power May Be Greater Than You Think

Very few people fully realize the power of the police. Young people, and not-so-young people, say, "Why can't I say or do what I want when I'm not causing any trouble? So what if I call the cops a few names or give them the finger. What can the cops do?"

The honest answer is that the police can do just about anything they want to do. Some people, who perhaps have watched too much television, think they can yell threats or curse at an officer and get away with it. After all, he or she is a "servant of the people." But police do not have to accept crude and rude behavior from anyone.

If you react to questioning by an officer with curses or threatening gestures, the officer may decide that a show of power is needed to get your cooperation. You could suddenly find yourself handcuffed and sitting in a squad car or detained for several hours at the police station. Later the case might be dismissed, but nothing is likely to happen to the officer. Even if you file a complaint, that officer was well within his or her rights. Make no mistake: Police have power and they use it.

CHAPTER 3

Juveniles and the Justice System

Minor Age, Major Problems

Public opinion and the laws of most states consider a young person's eighteenth birthday as the date he or she becomes an adult. At age eighteen people are responsible for their actions, since they have then reached the age of majority. Anyone younger is called a minor or a juvenile. Legal age for marriage, joining the military, voting, etc. varies by state. Check with the office of the state attorney general for specific ages governing emancipation laws in your state.

Many years ago the misbehavior of a juvenile was handled almost entirely by family or school officials, especially in smaller towns and rural areas. Police were rarely involved unless the crime was murder, serious personal injury, or major theft of property or money. If police did get involved, the case became a major news item and the young person was confined in adult prison and tried in regular court.

Times changed. More and more young people moved to large cities where neighbors did not know them or their families. When neighbors were bothered by a young person, they called the police.

Action by the police often created a dangerous situation for a juvenile. A fifteen-year-old first-time shoplifter might find himself thrown into a common cell with adult criminals. A hungry teen who stole food might be given the same punishment as an adult thief.

Socially-conscious citizens began to insist on separate holding facilities and separate courts for young offenders. The result was widespread growth in juvenile and family courts and juvenile holding centers. The emphasis of these courts was not on punishment or jailing, but on support for the young person, to give him or her the chance to be a good citizen.

Tried as Juvenile = Let off Easy

Do you think the above equation is true? Do you, like many young people, believe things like, "It doesn't matter what I do until I'm eighteen"?

From *The Washington Post*, May 7, 1993:

"One high school freshman arrested in Rockville six weeks ago said he would stop his spray painting only 'if my hands got cut off.'

"He said he's confident that having a criminal record will not hurt his future because 'it'll be erased when I'm eighteen. Besides,' he added, 'the artistic skill could help me get into college.'"

We've all seen a lot of spray-painted signs and highway overpasses. Whether this young man's talents will get him into college is beside the point. If he is concerned about his future he needs to know how the police and courts are changing their treatment of juveniles:

- The emphasis is shifting from reform to punishment.
- Misbehaviors seen not too many years ago as pranks are viewed more seriously today.
- The juvenile's name might be published in the local paper, and if his or her case were to go to court, it could be open to the public, including reporters.
- Juvenile records are *not* erased when someone becomes an adult.

Why Have Times Changed Again?

In recent years, more than a million young people have been arrested each year. The number keeps rising. For example, the FBI reported that 633,152 youths under the age of eighteen were arrested in the United States in 1990. Four years later that number had more than tripled to 1,988,982 teens arrested in 1994.

Those numbers are almost too big to believe. This increase in juvenile crime worries many citizens. People are concerned that juvenile courts are "too soft" on young offenders and that minors are not properly punished. Some people worry that the courts are not doing enough to stop the increase in violent crimes. For these and other reasons, citizens are calling for a greater crackdown on juveniles for both small and major crimes.

What's in the Future?

More and more young people are likely to be involved with the justice system in the coming years, not only for crimes but also for behaviors that were excused or ignored by police and the public in the past. As the crime rate continues to rise, many states have made novel attempts at reducing juvenile crime with remedies such as boot camps, outdoor experiences, lectures by convicts, and scare tactics that involve locking up first offenders for a few hours.

One of the methods being considered in Indiana, Pennsylvania and in Maryland is based on an old tribal custom of the Maori people of New Zealand. A police officer presides when the victim and his or her family meet with the offender and family. The group decides how the victim should be compensated. Traditionally known as a shaming ceremony, this practice is intended to make the crime personal for the one who did it.

Some states have recently begun to publish the names of juvenile offenders in the paper. You can also expect in the near future to see more news stories about juvenile offenders on television. These kinds of exposure may make present or future job-hunting more difficult for young people who break the law.

In the past, court records of juveniles were hard to obtain. Releasing the names and records of juvenile offenders to the public is now becoming common. Juvenile records are already being made available in some areas to support a request for harsher punishment of an adult with a long record as a juvenile offender. A juvenile record can also cause a young person to be tried as an adult while, in terms of age, still a juvenile. For example, one fifteen-year-old had prior theft charges. When he beat up another boy, he was said to be a danger to the community. Because of his previous criminal record, he was tried as an adult and was subject to adult laws and punishments.

Even in those states where records are not open to the public, the records can be accessed by court order. A record as a juvenile can follow someone, for example, into the armed forces.

Because of the great impact on a young person's future, the most important person in the judicial chain is a minor's first contact—the police.

Minors and the Police

The police, as the enforcers of our laws, often find themselves with choices to make when young people are involved. These choices are not the same ones that confront the officer when he or she deals with an adult.

Why are the choices different? Because civil rights laws do not apply to minors in quite the same way they do to adults. A pamphlet put out by the Bar Association of Montgomery County, Maryland, states, "Juveniles are entitled to most but not all of the constitutional rights and safeguards guaranteed to adults." In other words, the rights of minors are more limited and less clear-cut than those of adults.

At the present time, in most places in the United States, the police can arrest or take into custody a minor if they suspect that the young person

- is being abused or neglected,
- is being encouraged to commit criminal acts, and/or
- is suspected of committing a crime.

In most cases, if a juvenile is picked up by the police, the police have judged that one or more of these three conditions exist. No proof is required.

Why can the police arrest or question a young person without solid proof? Because our laws entrust communities to take care of every child, no matter how he or she behaves. In turn, communities expect the police to watch out for the welfare of the young. Let's look at each of the three conditions.

Juvenile Abuse or Neglect

"My name is Christy. My brother is a little wild. He goes to a high school for kids with problems, and he's been arrested a couple of times. I guess he gets it from our dad, who's a control freak. Anyway, my dad was always yelling and beating up on me, and my brother picked on me. They called it teasing, but sometimes what they did really hurt. They just laughed when my mom and I cried and yelled.

"One afternoon my brother burned my arm in several places with a cigarette. The next day a teacher noticed the burns and took me to the nurse. They called in the assistant principal. She called the police. The officer brought a social worker with him. I got scared and told them everything that goes on at home.

"I was put in a foster home. My foster mom and dad are real nice to me. I still love my real family and hope I can move back home soon. But for now, life is a lot calmer and I'm happy not to be hurt anymore."

When any minor is picked up because the officer believes that the young person is abused or neglected, various agencies of the police and courts join forces. Their job is to help create the best possible conditions for the young person so that he or she will not be abused or neglected. Their first goal is to take care of the young person. However, because many people believe that abuse and neglect drive young people to commit crimes, a second goal is to prevent future crimes from happening.

The social workers and probation officers who work with the courts first talk with the young person. They try to help him or her get a fair deal within the legal system and better living conditions. Perhaps the young person needs help at home. Maybe a different school would be the answer. Whatever it is, the juvenile division and the social workers try to help. These workers have saved many young people from bad living conditions, a poor school setting, or possible criminal behavior.

Unfortunately, the government does not always fund these child-care programs adequately. Poorly trained people are sometimes hired, and serious mishandling of cases does occur.

Encouragement to Commit Crimes

Because some adults do not know about laws that apply to minors, they permit minors to commit acts that are cause for arrest. For example, if an adult gives you, as a minor, alcohol or cigarettes, you are both breaking the law. Some adults persuade minors to commit serious crimes for them because they believe laws and punishments for minors are less severe. Every young person should be aware that when you break laws, you are subject to arrest and so is the adult who assists you. And you could be tried as an adult.

Suspicion of Committing a Crime

The police don't go looking for juveniles to arrest. But as more young people commit acts with serious consequences, more demands are made by the community on the police to help deal with juvenile misbehavior.

> Let's suppose Tiffany, fifteen, and Joe, her sixteen-year-old boyfriend, decide to cut their afternoon classes and drink beer in his car in the school parking lot. When the last bell rings, Tiffany jumps on the hood of the car and yells, "Let's go for a ride!" With Tiffany spread-eagled over the windshield, Joe laughs as he drives the car recklessly around the parking lot. Suddenly, another student dashing to catch her bus is hit by the car. Her leg is broken. What do you think happens to Joe and Tiffany?

- Because the incident happens on school grounds, school administrators handle the case and the police are not called.
- Tiffany is not responsible because she is under age.
- Both are minors, and as such, cannot be arrested by the police.
- Because Joe was driving, he will go to trial and eventually get a much more severe punishment than Tiffany.

We can't tell you how the story of Tiffany and Joe ends, because its outcome depends on the state and the particular school at which it happened. What is important about the case is that more than ever in U.S. history, schools now look to the police for support and help.

More and more communities are asking, "Where do schools fit into the realm of law enforcement?"

Public School Does Not Mean Open to the Public

Casual visitors are not welcome in schools anymore. Even though schools are public buildings, they are run for the students. Even if you once attended a school, you are no longer free to enter the school and roam around. Access to schools is tightly controlled in most places. In city high schools, entrances often contain metal detectors, and security guards regulate entry.

You may have a good reason for visiting a school. Be sure to check in at the main office and get a pass before walking around the building. If a principal or assistant principal says you can't visit at that time, leave quietly. If you are asked to leave and you don't, you are trespassing and can be arrested.

Schools, often backed by state law, also have the right to insist that no weapons, pagers/beepers, or cellular phones be brought into the school. Students who violate these rules are subject to school discipline and perhaps even arrest. Nonstudents and visiting adults are definitely subject to arrest if they bring weapons into a school. As technology changes, the laws that govern electronic devices are changing. Contact the school and ask about their regulations before carrying any electronic device into the school itself.

School Searches

Another issue that has brought police into schools is the matter of drugs and the rights of students.

Greg is a drug dealer. He wants Dominick to help him by delivering some of his deals. He goes to Dominick's school, which Greg had attended until he dropped out. He slips into the school without getting permission and heads for the gym, where he knows Dominick has class during the last period of the day.

Would the school principal search Greg if he or she saw him in the halls? Not likely. If the principal suspected Greg had drugs, he or she would call the police at once. Dominick is a different case. Since he is still in school, the principal might call him into the office if someone thought Greg had given him drugs. Principals and assistant principals have the right to search a locker if they have good reason. In fact, they can search all the lockers in a school if they have reason to do so. In many places, they also have the right to search a student. If you are a student and a principal or assistant principal wants to search you, you have the right to request that another adult be present. This is not only for your protection but for the protection of the administrator as well. If a witness is not present, remind the administrator of this right before a search begins. In most school systems, however, *teachers* cannot open a student's locker or search the student unless that student gives permission.

The Community, Juveniles, and the Police

Like schools, other segments of the community are now looking to the police to aid in crime prevention and to keep first offenders from going on to more serious crimes. Until recent times, young people have rarely been arrested and punished for pranks such as vandalism, graffiti, and loud noisy behavior unless they hurt someone or damage property. Although laws have been on the books, teachers, parents, neighbors, the business community, and the police have tended to ignore them or warn offenders and their parents. Only major incidents involved the police and made headlines in the news.

But as the cost of mischief goes up, many communities are cracking down on minor thefts, rowdy behavior, and graffiti. Graffiti in the form of hate messages gains public and police notice.

Here are some examples of what young people may see as harmless fun, but what the community and police may view as serious misbehavior:

- Students from one school tear down and steal the goalposts of their rival school the night before the big football game. The result? The county must use taxpayer money to replace the goalposts.
- Some young people gather every weekend at a fast-food place and sometimes talk loudly and have small fights. The result? Word gets around, and adults and other teens stop going there. The owner loses business because of this.
- Spray-painting is done on signs, bridges, schools, and other public places. The result? It costs money to remove graffiti. Some cities spend thousands of taxpayers' dollars every year to clean signs and buildings of graffiti.
- Stop signs and other traffic signs are stolen. The result? Drivers do not see a stop sign and drive through an intersection. Chances are that pedestrians or other motorists could be injured or killed in a car accident.

These criminal acts cause problems for a community and waste money. A very important result for a young person: Unhappy adults support courts that are tough on teens and young adults who commit acts of vandalism or mischief or are public nuisances.

Juveniles, Serious Crime, and the Police

The average adult's view of crime often depends on the age of the person committing the act. The police too, regardless of the law, often base their view of a young person's misbehavior on his or her age.

If you were a police officer, what would you do if you were called to the scene of a crime and saw that a four-year-old who found a loaded pistol had pulled the trigger and killed someone? What if the person was eight years old? Or sixteen years old? Or twenty-four years old? How does age affect the way the police handle the situation?

The younger you are, the less you are expected to know about right and wrong. Therefore, the law says that the younger the person is, the less responsible that child is for his or her own behavior. A very small child cannot understand the consequences of his or her actions, so the general rule has been that any child under age six or so is not able to commit a crime. In many instances, a very young child's misbehavior is treated as a "learning experience." The same behavior by a teen might be cause for arrest. Here are some examples of the problems of policing the behavior of young people:

Destruction of property
- A first-grader gets mad and puts glue all over several kids' notebooks. He will probably have to stay after school.
- A high-schooler gets mad at her ex-boyfriend and spreads glue on the seat of his new car. If he calls the police, she can be arrested.

Drugs
- A second-grader takes some of her mother's pretty pills to school to show friends. The pills would be taken away from the child and her mother called. The child might be suspended, and the mother would be warned to be more careful.
- A thirteen-year-old opens her locker at school and some of her illegal drugs fall out. The drugs are seized, and the parents and police are called. The police will probably arrest the girl. At the very least, she would be suspended from school.
- An eighteen-year-old is stopped while driving a car and is found to be carrying drugs. She will be arrested on the spot because she has reached the age of adulthood.

Sex
- A little boy and girl are caught playing "doctor." They are told not to do it and that certain body parts are private.
- A thirteen-year-old boy fools around sexually with a ten-year-old girl. He will probably be sent for counseling.
- An eighteen-year-old tries to force someone to have sex. The age or sex of the person who receives the attack doesn't matter. The police arrest him and may charge him with anything up to and including rape, depending on the circumstances.

Stealing
- A kindergartner who takes another child's pencil or lunch money will be scolded.
- A tenth-grader who steals a pen and watch from someone else's locker will be suspended from

school and may be charged with theft by the juvenile officers.

- An eighteen-year-old who takes a wallet from a
purse left in a grocery shopping cart will be arrested, have to go to court, and may receive a jail
sentence.

Although not all misbehavior causes the police to be
involved, certain actions are sure to trigger police
response. Juveniles caught doing any of the following face
serious consequences. These are serious crimes, no
matter what the person's age:

- Driving without a license or with a fake license
- Driving under the influence of drugs/alcohol
and/or causing an accident
- Carrying an illegal gun or illegal knife
- Selling drugs to minors
- Mugging
- Breaking into a house or store
- Stealing/robbery
- Having sex with a minor
- Rape
- Murder

These actions are crimes in any police officer's view. If
you commit one of them and you are a minor, you will find
yourself in real trouble. More so now than ever before,
your punishment can be harsh.

Remember: because of the complicated issues in juvenile justice, the police officer is the single most important
person in determining what happens to you. If you are
suspected of misbehavior, picked up for questioning, or
taken into custody, the officer will make many decisions
about you. Those decisions can affect your whole life.

One major study of the police, although done back in the 1960s, is still worth thinking about. It showed that, with the exception of offenders who had committed serious crimes or who were already wanted by the authorities, the arresting officer's handling of juvenile cases "depended largely on how a youth's character was evaluated by an officer." The youths taken into custody were those who "did not fit the officer's idea of normalcy."

Don't misunderstand us. The police are not looking for young people to haul into the station. But if you are confronted by the police and you behave in a way that convinces the officer of your good character, you won't regret it. In the next chapter, we talk about what to do if being good isn't good enough.

CHAPTER 4

Why Being Good Isn't Always Good Enough

Heavy rains over several weeks were causing flooding in some areas of the Southeast. The waters of the Potomac river came roaring down from the mountains on their way to the Chesapeake Bay. Seeing a chance to practice in serious white water, an Olympic-champion kayaker leaped into his craft and paddled east with the swirling currents.

Meanwhile, park police received word that a kayak had been spotted in the dangerous waters. Two officers set off to tell the person to get out of the water. By law, people must obey orders to get out of the water if the park rangers think the conditions are too dangerous. Rescues from the powerful Potomac are risky for the rescuers and expensive for the taxpayers, who must foot the bills for helicopters and rescue gear.

A video was taken as the first park police officer contacted the kayaker. The man had paddled over to the riverbank as ordered and was talking with the officer. He clearly felt that he should be allowed to practice his skills. The officer argued that he could not let anyone boat under such risky conditions. The second officer, impatient at the delay, came rushing down, slipped on the muddy bank, and fell into the water. Embarrassed and angry, the officer scrambled to his feet and yanked the bow of the kayak in the air and onto shore. The kayaker tumbled out.

Minutes later the kayak was seized and the man handcuffed and arrested.

Why the Police Stop Us

We may not like it if the police stop us because they think we are in danger. Most of us feel that we are the best judge of our own safety. Nor do we like it if the police stop us when we have broken the law. Nevertheless, we know that if police stop us for either of these reasons, they are only doing their duty.

However, we definitely do not like the police to question or hassle us if we don't think we are doing anything wrong or potentially dangerous. We consider this unreasonable police action. Yet police still do it.

Why Are Some People Stopped More Often Than Others?

Choosing to stop a person, for whatever reason, is in the judgment of the officer. Police have many reasons for making a stop and a great deal of leeway in judging whom to stop. Some people are stopped more often than others for three main reasons:

- People are stopped who might know something the police need to know.
- People are stopped because of stereotyping.
- People are stopped who match a profile.

Let's talk about each of these reasons.

People Are Stopped Who Might Know Something the Police Need to Know

Police sometimes stop people simply to get information. Good police work is based on knowing what is going on in the community. The police can stop anyone, anytime, if they believe he or she might have information that would help the police in their work. Who is doing what? Where are the trouble spots? Is this person who he says he is? When does this business close? How many people are at the concert? And so on. Information is an officer's most important weapon. Without accurate information, the police cannot keep the peace, protect the public, and catch lawbreakers.

People Are Stopped Because of Stereotyping

When Donnell glanced up, he saw a police officer come into the diner. He noticed that the officer glanced at him and the two women with him, and then he sat down with a cup of coffee at a nearby table. Donnell poked his finger into a piece of pizza as the two women in the booth continued to talk.

The first woman said jokingly, "It's 9:30 now. We're going to keep you here all night until you agree."

Donnell stalled and complained out loud.

At that point, the officer got up and walked over to their table. He smiled as he asked, "Everything all right here this evening?"

Both women nodded.

The second woman said, "We're just trying to convince this young man that he has too much going for him to drop out of school."

Donnell grinned and said, "Okay, I'll try again. I'll be in first period tomorrow, I promise."

The officer casually said, "Okay," and walked out the door, coffee in hand.

Donnell looked after him and said, "I guess he was wondering if two middle-aged white women were safe sitting in a diner with a black guy like me at this time of night!"

Do you think the officer who stopped to check out the threesome would have been as curious if the young man had been white? Or if the two women had been African Americans?

Some officers stop people based on appearance. They stereotype certain groups. That means they believe that people who look a particular way are "probably" the ones who cause trouble, or are "probably" planning to do something questionable, or are "probably" breaking the law.

Making such judgments on the basis of looks alone—whether the looks involve skin color, clothes, or the way people wear their hair—is a serious matter. Understandably people who are stopped on the basis of their looks feel unfairly targeted.

With long hair and a scruffy goatee, and dressed in grungy jeans and flannel, Larry looked like many people's idea of a rock musician. His long blond hair whipped about in the wind as he increased the speed of his old van. He was careful not to go more than ten miles over the speed limit. All the windows were open to keep him awake, since his last gig had finished around three AM in Pittsburgh.

Now he was on the turnpike driving down to Virginia Beach for an early gig that night. Suddenly, the flashing lights of a patrol car signaled him to pull over. He pulled off onto the shoulder at once.

"Just give me the ticket and let me get moving. I promise to pay it and to stay in the speed limit, even though I'm going to be late as it is," he said to the officer who had walked up to his vehicle.

The officer looked as if he had just stepped out of a shower. His uniform was spotless. His haircut was no longer than an inch. His face was clean shaven.

"Out of the car!" barked the officer. "Do you have any drugs on you?"

"Nope," Larry answered.

The officer didn't bother to reply, but started flinging Larry's bags, notebooks of music, and backpack out on the ground.

"You haven't got any right to search my stuff," Larry protested.

"Shut up," said the officer. "You drug-heads are all alike. You all ought to be locked up."

After thirty minutes of taking the van apart and finding nothing, the officer finally gave up. He gave Larry a ticket for speeding and a warning about resisting an officer. Larry was late for his Virginia Beach show.

What are the more common groups to be stereotyped? In no particular order, they are:

- young people
- males
- African Americans
- Hispanics
- Native Americans
- alcohol users
- drug users
- people with clothes and jewelry that are associated with gangs, drug use, pimps, or prostitution
- people sporting tattoos, unusual hairstyles, pierced body parts or other uncommon body decorations

People Are Stopped Who Match a Profile

Police most often stop people because of known information. They stop someone they think looks like a particular suspect or a potential victim. They stop people who match a description based on leads from witnesses about race, hair color, clothing, type of automobile, and so on. Such descriptions are called profiles.

From *The Frederick* (MD) *News-Post*, March 16, 1996:

"The masked man is described as white, about 5 feet 7 inches tall, weighing 140 pounds. In addition to the knit cap, he was wearing a gray hooded sweatshirt with two front pockets, blue jeans, and white Reebok sneakers."

Probable cause means that police have a good reason to do what they do. Profiles give police probable cause to stop certain people. And that person could be you.

Suppose the police report says that ten muggings have been committed by a red-haired man about eighteen years old, wearing a tan jacket and blue cap. If an officer sees you walking down the street—a young red-haired man wearing a tan jacket and blue cap—you will likely be stopped and questioned.

Sohana, an African-American teenager, liked to take a shortcut through the woods to go home after school. One afternoon a policeman stopped her as she came out of the woods. He asked her name, where she had been, where she was going, and whether she walked through the woods often.

Why did the officer stop Sohana? Just to hassle her because she was African American? No. The police had reports of a rapist hanging out in the woods who singled out young black women. The officer wanted to find out if she had seen any strange men. He had probable cause to warn her not to walk through the woods alone. Police use profiles to protect people as well as consider them suspects.

Other Examples of Probable Cause

- *You are in the wrong place at the wrong time.* The police have a report that teenagers are selling drugs in the late afternoon at Big Time Mall. You and your friends often hang out at Big Time Mall after school. An officer is likely to check why you are there so much.
- *You are with the wrong person at the wrong time.* You don't know it, but as you and a friend leave a store, she steals some tapes. The store owner sees

her and assumes that you have been shoplifting too. He calls the police. They stop you for questioning and search you.

- *You are a victim of gadget breakdown or carelessness.* As you walk through a parking lot, you see a new model of the XYZ car. You have wanted to get a good look at one, so you peer into the passenger side to see what the dash looks like. You touch the handle of the door, and the sensitive burglar alarm goes off. The mall police stop you as you start to walk away.
- *You break a law without knowing it.* You walk your dog in a park you have not been to before. You don't see the sign saying no dogs allowed. The police stop you.
- *You hang out after dark in a place where crimes often happen.* Most of the places listed below are policed more carefully after dark:
  — A mall parking lot
  — A fast-food parking lot
  — A park
  — A convenience-store parking lot
  — School grounds
  — A known drug-dealing area

Let's Face it—You're Likely to Be Stopped

As you can see, sooner or later you are likely to be stopped for one reason or another, good or bad. Two things you can do ahead of time help ease the situation and give you more control over what happens:

- Deal with your feelings about the police, especially if they are negative ones, before you have a police confrontation.

- Be prepared to identify yourself and to get help quickly if you need it by carrying proper identification.

Let's look at each of these ideas.

Deal with Your Feelings

A crowd of people gathered as an officer forced a moaning young man into a squad car. It seemed clear to them that the officer was arresting him without cause. They had seen no crime committed.

"Pig!" said one of the onlookers.

Others in the crowd shook their heads in disbelief.

The officer quickly closed the patrol car doors and moved on. He knew the crowd didn't realize that a few minutes earlier he had phoned a high school in his patrol area.

"I have a young man here—dark hair, about 5′6″ tall, 150 pounds. I can't get him to talk. Could he be a student of yours?"

"Yes, he is," the secretary had replied, with relief. "We just realized he was gone. Thank you so much."

The young man, who had severe emotional problems, had walked off the school grounds only minutes before the officer saw him, twirling down the median strip of the busy main street, his life clearly in danger.

The strong feelings everyone has about the police become especially important if you have an encounter with them. You will only add to your trouble if you send hostile messages, consciously or unconsciously.

The more you understand your attitude or your anger toward the police, and the reasons behind those feelings, the better prepared you are to deal with a stressful situation. Take the time to talk about negative feelings at home, in a class group, or with family or friends. Ask the local police/community relations officer to talk to your club or group. Most police departments welcome the opportunity to talk with citizens and explain their job.

Be sure to check out your own stereotypes too. The motorcycle officer who wears mirror glasses and never smiles may not win your "Officer Friendly" award, but give him or her a chance. You cannot judge how well an officer performs simply by noting his or her race, sex, or appearance.

Be Prepared to Identify Yourself

Right now stop and make a card to put in your wallet. This card should be in addition to the official ID card or driver's license that you carry at all times—when you are out biking, walking the dog, or simply hanging out. On the card, have the following two names and telephone numbers:

- Someone to call if you get into any kind of trouble. This person can be a parent, guardian, spouse, aunt, or other adult friend or family member— someone who keeps a clear head and gives sound advice. Write the telephone number clearly. Don't count on your memory. No matter how often you dial that number, when you are upset or confused or angry you may forget it.
- A lawyer whom you can call day or night. A lawyer who knows you and your family is best. If your family has limited finances, write the name and number of your local public defender's office.

What You Can Do to Improve Your Chances of Not Being Stopped

To avoid being stopped, your best bet is to obey the laws, especially traffic laws, to the letter.

Another good bet is to dress and act in ways that will help you be ignored by the police. Look clean and neat when you are out in public. This advice is especially hard for teens who want to dress and look different from adults. Many people, especially teens, feel it is their right to express themselves however they choose. Unfortunately, some people are unfairly stopped by the police solely because of their personal style and appearance. To get around this problem, some minority young people dress conservatively when they are on the street but carry other clothes with them.

From *The Washington Post*, March 29, 1996: "Driven to Extremes: When Chicago academic and journalist Salim Muwakkil hits the road, he employs a careful strategy gleaned from dozens of police stops: He rents a bland-colored Taurus, strictly obeys the speed limit, and definitely does not don his black beret. Muwakkil honed these techniques after . . . being stopped more often than he liked . . . for what he sardonically calls DWB—driving while black."

Many people, not just minorities, who want to avoid unnecessary stops by traffic officers, drive plain cars in dull colors. Red cars, flashy cars, sports cars, and muscle cars all can spell trouble to some police officers. You may want to avoid anything that will call attention to your car, or easily identify it, such as anti-police bumper stickers or vanity tags.

We are not talking about what is fair and right. If you have orange spiked hair and wear black leather from neck to toe, you may think that an officer who stops you and ignores the white-haired senior citizen in sneakers is being grossly unfair. We aren't saying that you're wrong in feeling that way. Prejudging anyone on the basis of appearance usually leads to an unfair result. But because the police, like all other people, make imperfect judgments at times, we want to give you tips and tricks for avoiding police encounters or minimizing them when they do occur. You may feel that conforming to a certain style of dress is not the solution to this problem. But by being aware of the situation, you can make an educated decision.

Stop, Look, and Listen

One veteran police officer says that most of the time people could avoid being stopped or questioned or hassled if they stop, look, and listen.

- STOP and ask yourself if what you are about to do is, or could look like, a crime. If so, don't do it. For example, don't hang around with someone who deals drugs or is a shoplifter. Don't try to get back at cranky neighbors by playing tricks on them. Don't fool around with burglar alarms.
- LOOK for possible trouble, and stay out of it. If you see a drug deal going on, don't go over to check out what happens. If you are headed for the local fast-food burger joint with a bunch of your friends and see a group of people with whom you've had trouble there already, pick a different fast-food place. Don't go out with a guy or girl who is a

known troublemaker, no matter how good-looking he or she is.

- LISTEN to the news on television and read newspapers. Learn where trouble spots are and stay away. If police say that gangs are hanging out on the corner of Risk and Rale Streets, don't even think of going there. If you hear that the old quarry has been the site of a couple of rapes, don't go there with a girlfriend or boyfriend. Keep your eyes and ears open. With common sense you can figure out the specific trouble spots in your city, town, or county where police are likely to be extra careful.

You Stopped, Looked, and Listened, But You Were Stopped Anyway

Marcos worked the night shift at the paper plant. During the day he went to school and worked out as a long-distance runner for the community college team. After being late to work several times, his boss told him flatly, "If you're late again, you'll be fired."

One evening Marcos left his apartment in plenty of time to get to work, but his car wouldn't start. He knew that if he ran he could get to work on time. With no time to change into his running shoes, he just headed across town.

Marcos knew that drug dealers hung out around the corner of Second and Duke Streets. To avoid the area, he cut down a back alley. Unfortunately, he popped out on Main Street just as a police car was answering a call to head to First National Bank. The report said that a dark-skinned man had robbed the bank. The minute the police saw Marcos running, they flipped on their lights and siren. Moments late, they were out of their car with pistols drawn. Marcos found himself handcuffed and shoved into the police cruiser. Eventually, his track coach and boss explained the situation, and Marcos was released with no charges.

Let's say that, like Marcos, you stopped, looked, and listened, but you still were stopped. When you are stopped by an officer for any reason, good or bad, your safety, civil rights, and maybe even your life depend on knowing how to react to what the officer says and does. The next chapter gives some practical tips on dealing with any confrontation.

CHAPTER 5

If You're Stopped

As the rain beat down, Juan turned his windshield wipers up to high. With headlights on and sticking to the speed limit, he drove very carefully to the mall and parked exactly between the lines. In the United States only six months, he had no wish to find out about police here. He knew about police in his own country, and he didn't want any trouble.

Juan jumped out of his car and made a run through the heavy rain. The storm swirled about him. Suddenly, he was aware that a police officer was chasing him and yelling, "Stop! Stop!"

Juan panicked. He ran harder. He didn't know what he had done, and he didn't want to find out. Maybe he could lose himself in the crowd. But as he grabbed at the mall door, he felt the officer grip his coat and hold him tightly. Juan turned around and threw his hands over his head.

"Cool it, man," said the officer. "I just wanted to give you back your wallet. You dropped it when you got out of your car. Check and see if everything is in it. If not, I'll go back with you and help you look. I've got a flashlight."

Through television, newspapers, magazines, and the Internet, stories about the police often spread to all parts of the world. These stories most often show police as brutal and dangerous to anyone who has dealings with them. It is true that reports of police brutality have steadily climbed as the rate of crime has risen. The majority of the police, however, use only the power needed to keep the community safe.

Unfortunately, the few bad ones are more newsworthy. They cause the rest of the officers to receive undue blame and hatred. But the bad ones are the ones we hear about and worry about. When police stop us, we are often confused about how to react. We may be frightened and feel threatened, too, as we size up the officer and the situation. We wonder, "Is this one of the dangerous ones?"

What is the police officer thinking when he or she stops you? You can bet that, because of his or her experience and training, the officer is also sizing you up.

More than 150 police officers are killed each year in the line of duty. Many times the officer is killed while making a routine stop for questioning. The officer who detains you doesn't want to become a statistic. At the very least, then, when an officer stops you, he or she wonders if you are dangerous.

So any encounter with an officer is likely to have both of you feeling edgy.

What's Under Your Control?

What happens during a confrontation depends on many things:

- The police officer
- The circumstances and seriousness of the incident
- What you say and do

While the officer is sizing you up and deciding how to handle the situation, the only thing you can really control is what you say and do. What you say, how you say it, your body language, and what you don't say will all play a part in the outcome of the encounter.

You and a friend have been hanging around Burger Boy for two hours, hoping more of your friends will stop by. You walk around the parking lot for a while. Then you lean on the hood of your friend's car and talk. Still no one shows. Suddenly a police officer walks around the corner of the building and turns a light on the two of you. What do you suppose the officer's reaction would be in each of the two following scenarios?

Cop: "Hi. Car problem?"
Friend: "So what's it to you? We got a right to be here. Don't give us a lot of crap!"

Cop: "Hi. Car problem?"
Friend: "Nope, Officer. Just waiting for some friends. Guess they're not going to show. You want us to move on?"

The Golden Rule

Your behavior tells the officer how you want to be treated. If you are polite, most officers will be polite in return. If you talk tough, you can be in for a long confrontation. If you act tough, or if you act threatening, the officer has every right to use whatever force is necessary to defend himself and take you to the station.

Whenever an officer walks up to you, feel out the situation: Is the officer clearly trying to be friendly? Does he look relaxed? Then lighten up and act friendly too, or at least be pleasant. Being pleasant means greeting the officer verbally. Saying "hi" is enough.

Is the officer smiling, but doesn't look as if she means it? Is her face tight and angry? Be alert to signs that the officer is ready to explode. If so, be careful what you say and do.

Even if the officer seems relaxed, the language you use can turn a calm situation into an explosive one. When you're with your friends, you may not think much about using swear words. If you use such language with a police officer, you may as well toss a lighted match into a gas tank. Police do not expect you to use offensive language, even if they use it themselves. Don't call an officer a "pig" or worse. Some even dislike being called a cop. Stick with the word *officer*.

We realize that some of you may resent this "Yes, officer" approach to dealing with the police. It may sound as if we are suggesting that you should go out of your way or make extra efforts in the event of a police encounter. We won't argue with you on that point. Mainly, though, we are noting that simple good manners can give you a very necessary edge in such a situation.

If the officer insults you or calls you names, stay cool. Think, "Am I doing anything to make the officer act tough?" If not, relax and do or say only what the officer asks, no matter how foul his actions or words. Now is not the time to let him know you think he is a pig. If you start to lose your temper, take a deep breath before you speak.

Some Practical Guidelines for Confrontations

When an officer wants to talk with you:

- *Don't run away!* Don't even turn away or walk away. The officer may consider you armed and dangerous. You could get shot. Don't take a chance. Stand still.
- *Give him or her a chance to speak.* If you are with friends, lay off the smart remarks, the swear words, and the tough talk. Stand quietly, but relaxed.
- *Stay about three feet away from the officer.* Never crowd his or her personal space. You don't have to move if he or she moves closer to you unless you are uncomfortable. Don't try to shake hands unless the officer offers his or her hand.
- *Maintain eye contact.* Look the officer directly in the eye both while you are talking and when you are listening. If that is hard for you, fix your gaze at a spot in the middle of his or her forehead.
- *Keep your hands in plain sight.*
  - DON'T reach in your bag or backpack without permission from the officer, not even to get a tissue to wipe your nose.
  - DON'T put your hands in your pockets.
  - DON'T use your hands in such a way that the officer might think you have a gun.
  - DON'T use either hand in such a way that the officer might think you are making an obscene gesture.
  - DON'T touch the officer or make any fast moves with your hands.

- *Don't joke.* Never pull a toy gun or even joke that you have a gun. If you have a nervous laugh that is hard for you to control, be especially careful. You may even want to say, "I'm sorry. I laugh when I'm nervous."
- *If the officer asks, give your name and address and say where you are going.* In many places, you may be arrested if you don't.
- *Give only the information you are asked for.*
- *Tell the truth.*

If you answer questions politely, the officer most likely will move on. On the other hand, if you give the officer cause for anger, you could be cooling off in the police station just because of your attitude.

On the Road

We live in a mobile world, so the police are more likely to stop you in a car than elsewhere. From the officer's point of view, this is a highly dangerous situation because he or she cannot see everything that you and the others in the car are doing or what weapons you may have. Every time an officer stops someone in a car, that officer risks his or her life.

> You have been stopped by the police for speeding. The officer walks toward your car window. Which of these ways of handling the problem do you think would work best?
> Officer: You were doing thirty miles over the limit.
> You (jumping out of car): Like h—I was. You're out of your mind.
> or

Officer: You were doing thirty miles over the limit.

You (with hands on wheel): I was thinking about my job. I just didn't notice how fast I was going. Sorry.

or

As the officer walks to your car, you stamp on the gas pedal and take off as fast as your wheels will travel. You spin gravel in the cop's face as you hit the pavement.

The most important rule when you are driving a vehicle is: Stop when you are asked to stop! If you don't, you make the officer wonder whether you have done something wrong. If you take off and try to outrun the officer, he or she is sure you have done something wrong, like stealing the car, and will stop you one way or another.

Remember, don't try to outrun the police even if

- you are speeding,
- your license has expired, and/or
- you have alcohol or drugs in the car.

Settle for the ticket and/or punishment. Don't make things worse.

Franklin lost his wallet with his driver's license in it. He planned to get a new one sooner or later, but somehow hadn't gotten around to it yet. One day, he took his uncle's car without permission. His uncle, not knowing Franklin had taken the car, reported it stolen.

Franklin was driving through town when he heard a siren behind him. He knew he would be grounded by his dad if he got caught, so he tried to outrun the squad car. After a chase at speeds up to 100 miles an hour, he crashed into a wall as he tried to make a turn.

He was charged with malicious destruction, one count of theft, unsafe lane changing, driving without a license, driving the wrong way on the highway, negligent driving, reckless driving, and fleeing and eluding police in a motor vehicle.

If he had stopped when told to, he would have had only one count of speeding and one count of driving without a license. His uncle could have cleared up the stolen-car part. Franklin ended up in court with major restrictions on his life.

Police cars are equipped to outrun just about any other vehicle on the road. Besides, the officer can always radio other cars to head off a runaway. Sadly, people are killed every year trying to outrun the police. Just as often, it is a person walking along the road or a child playing on the sidewalk who is killed.

From *The Washington Post*, April 13, 1996:
"Hit-and-Run Driver Kills Baby: A driver who police said was fleeing other motorists after a string of accidents raced into a residential neighborhood near Bladensburg yesterday, jumped a curb, and struck a woman walking with a toddler and pushing an infant in a stroller.

"The twenty-two-year-old woman and the toddler . . . were severely injured. The infant . . . died later despite frantic efforts to revive him. . . .

"Accident investigators drew a circle around each item they found and labeled it on the pavement with fluorescent orange spray paint:

"A baby bottle partially filled; a baby's sock; several yards away, another sock; a baby blanket; a toddler's black sneaker; an adult's white sneaker.

"The items were strewn in a ragged line along the path the car followed."

Tips if You're Stopped While Driving

Most of the same guidelines apply when you are stopped in a car as when you are on foot. In addition, when you are in a car and are pulled over, here's what to do:

- Put on your flashers the minute you see the police are trying to stop you. Wave your hand to show that you plan to stop.
- Slow down and bring your car to a safe stop as soon as you can. If you drive slowly with blinkers flashing, the officer will understand that you are looking for a safe spot, even if you have to drive some distance.
- When you have come to a full stop, set your emergency brake and put both your hands on top of the steering wheel. Leave your flashers on and turn on the dome light (the overhead light) if it is nighttime.
- If you are eating or drinking, stop. Give your full attention to what is happening.
- Turn off the radio, tape, or CD. Yelling back and forth over loud music will not help your case.
- Remind the others in your car not to make any sudden moves and to keep their hands where the officer can see them.
- Don't get out of your car unless the officer tells you to do so. If you are a female, alone, and are

stopped on a deserted road, be polite but express your concern about getting out of your car. Offer to follow the officer to the nearest station. An officer will not ask you to get into his car for a simple traffic ticket.

Reach for It

You will be asked for your driver's license and the car registration. Be sure you have both with you at all times. Are you tempted to make a quick trip to the store without bothering to find your license or registration? Don't take the chance. A police officer may be watching if you slide through a stop sign! If you borrow a car, ask about the registration. Some drivers keep it in the car, but many people prefer to keep it in their wallet.

Don't drive with a phony license. A phony license may get you a drink in a bar, but it won't help if you are stopped. If you don't have a valid license, you are in big trouble. In most places, you would not even be allowed to drive your car home. Someone would have to come get you from the station.

Wait until you are asked for your license or registration to reach for it. When you reach for it, do so slowly. If it is in your pocket or the glove compartment, say so as you reach for it.

Remove your license from your wallet before giving it to the officer, or the officer might suspect you of attempted bribery.

Gun Control

Don't ever give an officer any reason to think you are reaching for a gun. Hold a backpack in such a way that the officer can see into it when you reach in. Similarly, a woman should hold her purse open in full view when reaching for a license. Make no sudden moves. Give the officer no reason to be concerned about the outcome of what should be a routine stop. You don't want to fool with an edgy officer who has a handgun ready.

If you are very nervous, prop your hand on your other arm or on the car door to avoid trembling while you wait for the officer to take your license. A shaking hand may be viewed as a sign of guilt, possibly about something else—like a hidden gun.

Drugs and Alcohol

If you have illegal drugs or alcohol with you, don't try to hide them or throw them away. If you have drugs, don't try to swallow them. More than one person has died from swallowing packets to get rid of them. Tell the others in your car not to try it either. A drug charge is not worth dying for. Besides, from the minute an officer decides to stop you, he or she will watch your every move and will see you trying to get rid of the drugs.

If an officer thinks you've been drinking, he or she may ask you to take a breathalizer test. You should know that in some states refusal to take a sobriety test may result in automatic suspension of your license.

Don't Dream up Excuses

If you are stopped for speeding, don't bother to argue or make an excuse unless you are transporting a critically ill person to medical care and time is crucial. Tears seldom help either. Police have heard every excuse you can think of. If you sincerely express you're sorry, you may receive only a warning.

If you have a legitimate explanation, ask the officer to write it down on his or her report of the incident. You'll probably still get a ticket, but if the case goes to court, your explanation will be on record, and the ticket may be thrown out by a kindhearted judge.

Don't even think of trying to pay off the officer or threaten him or her with the name of some powerful politician.

> After days of trying to untangle the traffic tie-ups caused by huge snowfalls in a northeastern city, an exhausted police officer yelled at a woman to move her car. The driver was slow in doing so, and when she finally pulled her car to the curb, he kept yelling at her. When the car stopped, she jumped out and said to the officer, "F—you. You don't have to be so obnoxious about it." The officer lost his cool.
>
> The woman ended up at the police station with cuts on her neck that she said she received when the officer grabbed her throat. She also reported that her right hand and wrist were sore because the officer had clamped the handcuffs too tightly.
>
> Witnesses for both parties reported different versions of what happened. But right or wrong, the woman was scheduled to appear in court the next month. How could this situation have been avoided altogether?

If you find yourself getting frustrated with the police officer, before you get angry, try the old trick of counting to ten. Then breathe in and do it again if you still feel angry. The minute you let anger control you, you have lost all control over the situation.

Don't swear or act hostile. The officer can be hostile too, and you will lose. Many times an officer has not planned to give a ticket, only a warning. But if you trigger the officer's ill will, you may get a ticket not only for speeding, but also for disorderly conduct, refusing to obey an officer, or another such offense. You may also be ordered out of the car and searched.

If You're a Passenger

As a passenger in a routine traffic stop, you may be thinking that it's the driver who has committed the traffic offense, so you have nothing to worry about. A recent Supreme Court ruling, however, states that when a vehicle is stopped, all its occupants are being stopped. The Supreme Court ruled that police officers may order a passenger out of any car they stop for routine traffic violations, even in the absence of reason to suspect that a passenger has committed a crime.

The powers of the police have been extended to protect officers on patrol.

Searches and Seizures

If an officer asks to search you or your car, you can say no. Say it firmly, but not with anger. If the officer searches you and/or your car anyway, take careful mental notes of what the officer says and does. Don't attempt to stop the officer.

There are times to fight for your rights, but this isn't one of them. Save your case for court or for making a complaint through official channels. Later in this book we'll tell you how to do that. Mouthing off about your rights at the time of a search can only make matters worse.

If police find illegal drugs or alcohol on you or your friends, don't try to explain it away. Whatever you say may be used against you. If you are arrested, you will have your chance later to tell your side of the story.

The police can take your car even if the drugs are not yours. If they do, don't argue. Just do what you are told. Never forget, at the time of a search, the police have ALL the power.

Think of it this way. Let's say you start to cross a street in the crosswalk. You look up and see an eighteen-wheeler coming straight for you at ninety miles an hour. Would you hold up your hand and tell the truck driver you have the right of way? Or would you jump out of the way? Of course you would jump out of the way.

In the same sense, jump out of the arresting officer's way by not fighting back, no matter what the officer says or does. If you get physical with the officer, he or she can, by law, use even more force. If you physically demand your rights at the wrong time, you have a greater chance of getting hurt.

Most times when you are stopped by the police, they will be polite if you are. After all, an officer who stops you when you are speeding is just doing a job. You don't have to like the police or what they do to understand that usually they just do what they are paid to do—like the rest of us.

For some of us, however, personal problems may make our situation more difficult if we are stopped.

If You Have a Learning Disability

Ben had left an empty can of beer on the floor of his

car. When he was stopped, he fumbled and fussed and fumed when he couldn't find his license and registration after the officer asked for them. Spying the beer can, the officer suspected that Ben had been drinking. He asked a few questions that would have been easy for most people, but which Ben had trouble answering. When the officer asked if he had been drinking, Ben chose to ignore his learning problem, as he tried to do around his friends.

"F—you. I'm not drunk, damn it," Ben roared.

What do you think happened to Ben?

Do you have a reading or learning disability that may keep you from doing as the officer says? Your learning problems may get in the way if you are asked to do any one of the following:

- Find your identification and the car's papers ("I need to see your driver's license and registration.")
- Follow multiple-step directions ("Please turn around, put your hands above your head against the wall, and stand with your feet apart.")
- Do academic-type tasks ("Recite the alphabet backwards.")
- Answer questions accurately, especially those that involve direction ("Did you say the other car was coming east on Third Street?")
- Do tasks that require good motor skills ("Walk that yellow line, one foot in front of the other.")

In addition, people with learning disabilities often become confused, frustrated, and angry when under stress. A simple question ("Isn't this a school day for you?") may trigger a blowup that makes the officer suspect the person is hiding a more serious problem. Unless their background includes experience with learning disabilities, police officers may not recognize the signs of this problem.

The moment an officer stops you is the time to make the officer aware of your problem. Since learning problems are not easily seen, the outcome of the confrontation depends even more on your proving your problem to the officer right up front. If you have a reading or learning disability, ask your doctor for a card that explains your problem. The card should name your disability, explain the particular problems you have, and give the name and phone number of the doctor who can vouch for your difficulty.

Another option is to carry a card signed by an educator. This could be the principal of your school or the reading or special education teacher who works with you. A card signed by school staff will probably not carry as much weight as one signed by a medical doctor, however.

Carry this card with you in your wallet, next to your driver's license. Then tell the officer about your learning problem. Be polite. Be courteous. Don't sound as if the learning disability should be an excuse for what you did, but be ready to explain the problems it can cause.

Other Special Problems

Do you have special medical problems, such as an orthopedic problem, cerebral palsy, or any other neurological problem that might cause you to walk with a stagger or pass out? Police often assume that people who stagger or fall down are drunk. They have been known to disbelieve suspects who protested that they were not drunk or on drugs. If you have such a problem, make and carry a card like the one described above. It must be signed by your doctor to prove your disability.

Anyone who is profoundly deaf or does not speak English should also carry a card signed by a doctor or other authority. This card should certify that the bearer does not understand spoken English words. Because many people have tried to fool officers by pretending to be a foreigner or a person who is deaf, police tend to be suspicious of anyone who claims not to understand.

"Have a Good Day and Watch Your Speed"

If both of you have dealt well with the encounter, the officer will deal swiftly with your traffic violation. You may or may not get a ticket, and you'll both go on your way.

"You're Under Arrest!"

But what if the police decide to arrest you? What can you expect to happen? We'll tell you in the next chapter.

CHAPTER 6

Arrested!

Robert was determined not to be involved with the police, either as a victim or a suspect. He lived in a large city, so he always put a device on his steering wheel to deter thieves. One evening, however, after a movie with his girlfriend, the key to the device broke off as he tried to unlock it. He walked his girlfriend home, returned to the car with a saw and crowbar, and began to free the steering wheel. Suddenly lights flooded him and his car. Police surrounded him, guns drawn. Arrested! He had never dreamed it would happen to him.

Because Robert tried not to break the law, he had good reason to think he would never be arrested. Even young people who knowingly break the law seldom expect to be caught and arrested. But if they have committed a serious crime, they probably will be.

You may be saying to yourself that you know people who are drug runners or who have sold stolen electronic equipment for a long time and they haven't been caught. For now, you're right. Police often leave small offenders alone, even if they know who they are and what they're doing. They expect the minor criminals to lead them to the major criminals. When small offenders quit being useful to the police, they are then arrested.

Other people who do not expect to be arrested are those who, knowingly or not, help friends break the law or are at the scene of a crime.

Can You Be Arrested if You Help Someone Commit a Crime?

Yes. You are an accessory accomplice if

- you know about a crime before or after it takes place, or
- you help the person before or after the crime.

In either case, you can be arrested unless you report the crime.

You do not have to be near the scene of a crime to be considered an accomplice. Although you may have a number of reasons for going along with a plan to commit a crime, don't buy into any of them. Committing a crime because you are afraid of the person who asks you or because you love that person is not smart. Think through what might happen. Know that the responsibility for the crime rests with you as well as with the person who carries it out.

A fifteen-year-old girl gave her boyfriend a family hunting knife when he asked for it. She saw that he was upset and knew he had emotional problems. But she loved him, and she was also a little afraid of him when he was angry. That night he used the knife to kill someone.

What do you think will happen to her?

- She will be tried as an adult and could face life in jail.
- She will be tried as a juvenile, with a short time in jail possible.
- She will be questioned but not taken into custody because she didn't know what her boyfriend had planned to do.

In this case, the teenager was charged as an accessory accomplice in the slaying. A judge denied her request to be treated as a juvenile, and she will be tried as an adult. This ruling means she could face life in prison.

If You're at the Scene of a Crime

If you are at the scene of a crime, you are automatically a principal accomplice. Unless you report the crime, you can be arrested.

You are driving around with a friend in your car. Involved with talking, you notice that your speed has crept up fifteen miles over the limit. Just then you hear the police siren. You don't want a ticket—but hey, you were speeding. So you pull over, keep your hands on the steering wheel, and figure you'll just have to live with the fine. As the officer walks toward your car, it dawns on you that your friend has been smoking pot. The odor of it fills the car, even though your friend is no longer smoking. You slowly roll down your window to give the officer your license and registration.

What will happen next?

- You and your friend will both be arrested for drug possession.
- The officer will impound your car.
- The officer will give you a warning and a wink and let you go.
- You will get only a speeding ticket.
- The officer will consider you guilty and arrest you both.

What Happens in an Arrest?

If the officer finds grounds for arrest, he or she might say something like this while handcuffing you:

"I am placing you under arrest. Before I question you, I must tell you that you have the right to remain silent. Anything you say can be held against you. You may choose not to answer any questions until you have a lawyer present. If you can't afford a lawyer, one will be provided for you."

Here are two questions young people often ask:

- *Will my rights always be read to me?* Whether you are an adult or a juvenile, you are supposed to be told your rights, but not until and unless a police officer says you are under arrest. The younger you are, the less likely they are to read you your rights. If the officer does not read you your rights but starts asking questions about a crime, ask politely if you are being arrested. If the officer says yes, say that you choose not to answer any more questions. The officer may get angry, but this is your right. Stay civil, but stay quiet.

- *What should you do while your rights are being read to you?* Listen politely and quietly. No attitude.

Handcuffing

You will be handcuffed no matter why you are cited. Cited means being told that you will have to appear in court. Except for very young children, most police handcuff everyone they arrest. This practice is for their own protection as well as to keep you from escaping. In some places, it is the law.

You may have your hands cuffed in front of you or behind you. You are not likely to have your legs cuffed together unless you fight and struggle with the officer.

Try not to struggle while you are being handcuffed. The more you struggle, the more likely the officer is to put the cuffs on very tightly. If you squeeze your fists tightly when handcuffs are being put on you, the cuffs may be a little more comfortable around your wrists when you later relax your fists.

Police Brutality—True or False?

It happens—less often than the news media would lead you to think, but more often than is right. What sometimes seems to an onlooker to be brutality is often legal and acceptable force, based on the resistance of the person being arrested. Police are required by law to use no more force than necessary to take a person into custody; therefore the more a person struggles, the more force the police may use.

Certain situations, however, seem to trigger brutality. A high-speed chase arouses the adrenaline in the officers doing the chasing. When the suspect is finally stopped, the pumped-up feelings of the officer might spill over into violent behavior unless the officer is very careful to exercise restraint.

Another situation that may trigger brutality on the part of an officer is the capturing of a person suspected of brutally raping or killing a child. The officer takes out on the suspect his or her own personal feelings about the crime.

If an officer takes you into custody, go quietly. In addition to that being the right thing to do, your calm and controlled behavior is less likely to trigger brutality. If you are treated with more force by the police than you feel was needed, check out the last chapter in this book on how to report police behavior to the authorities.

The Trip to the Police Station

If you are arrested by a police officer, you will probably be taken to the nearest station in the back seat of a police car. Ask the officer to fasten your seat belt for you if he or she forgets. Many of these cars are designed so that you cannot open the rear doors yourself.

If you and a lot of others are arrested at a concert or large gathering, you might be transported in a police van. If so, behave quietly and don't go along with others if they yell and scream or start trouble.

Do Police Ever Plant Evidence?

Yes, it has happened and probably will again. But it is not common. Police departments discipline officers who plant evidence or tamper with evidence. Well-trained police officers do not have to resort to such tricks to make good cases.

Guilty or Innocent, an Arrest Is an Arrest

When we left Robert at the start of this chapter, he found himself facing an arrest for breaking into his own car. Robert was able to clear himself because the manager of the movie theater knew him and helped him establish his identity with the police. His biggest problem now is finding a locksmith.

Let's say you are not quite as lucky as Robert. Let's say that, for whatever reason, you are cited. If you are an adult, you are now under arrest. As a juvenile, you would more likely be told that you are being taken into custody. Your parents may be asked to escort you to the police station or to meet you there.

Although the terms used to describe what happens to a juvenile and an adult are not always the same, the basic process is similar. Let's follow the arrest process and give you some tips to help you get through it.

The procedures associated with arrest, search and seizure, questioning, treatment at the station, and so forth have grown out of many years of experiences in law enforcement and the rulings of the courts.

These experiences and rulings are taught to officers at the police academy. They are required to follow arrest procedures. They are not going through a process just to annoy you or anger you.

Once you are under arrest, a series of actions is set in motion. You have little control over this process. The first phase of these actions ends only when you are released from the station or you are jailed until your court hearing.

At the Station

At the police station, you will be asked to empty your pockets and give the police any backpack, bag, or purse you may be carrying. Everything you give them will be listed on a form. You will be asked to sign a sheet saying that you confirm what they are holding. When you are released, you will get back everything except items that may be used as evidence. You will sign the sheet again to indicate that everything was given back to you.

Police procedures include keeping records. Officers collect a lot of information and make full reports about every arrest, every person arrested, and the arresting officer. Information will be recorded as the arrest process continues.

Depending on why you are arrested, you may be searched. Strip searches are not common, but they do happen. In a strip search, an officer of your own sex checks all of your body openings to see if you are concealing anything. Being strip-searched by an officer of the opposite sex, except under highly unusual conditions, is cause for a serious complaint against the police after you are released.

After being searched, you will probably be photographed and may be fingerprinted.

Because the police do not want to risk a suicide, your shoes or shoelaces may be taken away, even if you are a juvenile. The same goes for belts, suspenders, ribbons, or any other type of string or rope.

If the police think there is reason to do so, you may also be tested for drugs or alcohol. Follow the directions carefully in taking the tests.

Let's assume you were read your rights at the time of arrest. You have another right at the police station. You are allowed by law to make one telephone call.

Get in touch with your parents, your legal guardian, your spouse, or a family lawyer. Your goal is to get the help you need, based on the act of which you're accused. For most juveniles, it is best to call your parents or another trusted adult. That person can help you decide whether you need a lawyer. If you decide together that you do, he or she can call the lawyer for you.

Juvenile or adult, everyone is entitled to be represented by a lawyer. If you do not have the money to pay an attorney, the public defender's office will help you fill out paperwork and obtain the services of a lawyer to represent you without charge. Use of a public defender is based strictly on finances. You must use—and pay—a private attorney if you are able to afford one.

Consider carefully before you involve a lawyer, however. We are often told that a person should say nothing until he or she has a lawyer. For a very serious crime, you definitely do need good legal advice. On the other hand, the wrong lawyer can turn a simple detainment into a complex problem. The National Association for the Advancement of Colored People (NAACP) gives some good advice: "It is suggested that a lawyer be called only after everything else fails or seems to be headed toward failure."

What Do You Say When You're Questioned?

If you didn't do anything, you should say so. Then keep quiet. That is your right, but sometimes it's not easy. However, think about what you are going to say before you speak. Police are trained to get answers that people don't want to give.

Say only what you must to answer questions simply and honestly. You don't have to say anything about matters related to the reason for your arrest. You have the right to refuse to say anything that might incriminate you; that is, indicate you are guilty. Tell the truth and answer reasonable questions about where you live, what you do, and so forth. Above all, don't say anything that might one day haunt you if it is taken negatively or out of context. This advice sounds easy. Trying to anticipate the long-term effect of your words is harder than it seems. We cannot urge you strongly enough not to talk excessively or giggle nervously. Do not volunteer information.

Darren had a way with words. He knew all the right words that people wanted to hear. He got along with his friends and with other students, who looked to him as a leader. He was captain of the school bas-ketball team. He had charmed parents and teachers as well as his classmates his entire life. "The gift of gab," one teacher said. "That's what you've got, Darren."

Late one Friday evening, Darren drove two friends to the top of a hill that overlooked the town. A case of beer was in the trunk. As the sun went down, the cans came out. Their laughing and talking and drink-ing was interrupted a few hours later by the lights of a police car.

His friends took off into the trees. "Big deal," thought Darren. "So they've caught me with a couple of empty beer cans. I can talk my way out of this."

At the station house, Darren quickly picked up the vibes from a very stern officer. He didn't want to squeal on his friends, but as he tried to find the words that would help his situation, he talked. And talked. And talked. His way with words got him informal supervision for ninety days. During this time he had to attend drug and alcohol lectures (and pay for them), watch a gory film on the horrors of drunk driving, and do community service work. Darren's gift of gab got him more than he expected.

Good Cop/Bad Cop Questioning

You have probably seen good cop/bad cop questioning on television. The first officer acts mean and threatening. The second officer acts friendly, supportive, and caring. The second officer may offer you coffee, soda, cigarettes, a snack, and so forth.

The goal of both officers is to get you to confess details about the crime. Remember to remain silent and answer only questions not related to the crime; for example, "What school do you go to?", "How old are you?", or "Where do you work?". Be careful what you agree to say on tape or to sign. Anything you say or sign may be used against you later in court.

Be Patient

The process in the police station can be slow. The police may be dealing with other more serious cases. They may be short-handed. A lot of paperwork must be done for every case. You may have to wait for a parent or lawyer to arrive.

Sometimes the police try to slow down the process. They hope you will get tired and anxious and confess to the crime.

Getting out

If you are a juvenile, you will probably be sent home with your parents unless the alleged crime is very serious.

What if your parents refuse to help you? The court can order them to take you home or can send you to a juvenile detention facility. Because fewer girls than boys are arrested, places to send females are more limited. A female might be sent to a detention center some miles from the station if she does not go home with a parent or guardian.

If you are an adult or will be treated as an adult, you may be locked in jail until your hearing. At a hearing, bail may be set for your release. Bail is money turned over to the court with the promise that you will show up in court when ordered. A bail bondsman will lend you the money to get out of jail if you or you family do not have it immediately available.

Dealing with the News Media

If the media express an interest in your case, we suggest that you say nothing. "No comment" works for politicians and movie stars, and it can work for you.

Do not alert newspaper, radio, or TV reporters to your case without checking with your family and a lawyer. Think about the pros and, more importantly, the cons of such media attention and what might happen. Many people, young and old, have caused themselves trouble when they tried to influence the press.

After Your Arrest

We can't tell you what will happen after the arrest process is complete. At that point, you will no longer be coping with the police. You will be involved in a completely different part of the criminal justice system—the courts. You will enter a confusing web of laws and lawyers, legal terms, and decisions that vary from state to state, based on the crime with which you are charged.

A long time will pass before you find your way out of this web. We can only say that the checks and balances within the justice system usually get the guilty prosecuted and keep the innocent from being persecuted.

The Downside of Arrest for Committing a Crime

First of all, obeying the law is the thing to do . . . because it is the right thing to do. But you also want to obey the laws because you don't need the hassle that comes from breaking the law and getting caught. An arrest is confusing and scary and makes you feel powerless.

What's more, if you're convicted of a crime, YOU WILL LOSE CONTROL OF YOUR LIFE FOR SOME PERIOD OF TIME. Other people will make the daily and long-term choices that you have always made about what you say and do. No hanging out with your friends, no taking off to catch a few rays at the beach or ballgame. Crime may pay in terms of immediate money, but not in terms of fun, peace of mind, and conscience. In addition, being convicted of a crime causes great pain to those who care about you, even if they have been in prison. You will be separated from the ones who need you and love you. You don't want that.

Family, friends, public agencies, and health clinics can help you solve your problems. Use their help to keep out of trouble with the police.

CHAPTER 7

Special Encounters

The labor union leaders had called a strike against a plant in a small city. A cold drizzle did not help the mood of the one hundred workers who gathered at the plant gate and awaited the results of one last negotiating session. After being on strike for two months, they were anxious to get back to work before winter set in.

Al Johnson, a husky young man, sneered at the police officers as they stood firmly in front of the gates of the plant. "Why don't we storm the building and show management who they're really dealing with?" he shouted.

"Yeah!"

"All-ll-rr-right!"

Other voices chimed in, and the police could see a riot brewing. Should they shoot? Strike out with clubs? Radio the state police for reinforcements? What to do? How bad would it get?

Suddenly Captain Weinberg stepped away from the gates and went up to Johnson. He stuck out his hand.

"Al, I hear your wife just had a baby boy. What great news. You're finally going to have a fishing buddy!"

Al grabbed the officer's hand and pumped it hard, his face one huge smile. For the moment, he totally forgot the strike. "Yeah, you gotta see him, Josh. He's fiesty. Gonna take after me, all right."

Then Al turned to the man beside him.

"Frank, I hear you just had a boy too! We're gonna win the football championship for sure—sixteen years from now."

Both men doubled over laughing.

Officer Weinberg slapped Al on the shoulder and moved through the crowd swiftly, talking to men he knew to be leaders. He asked about ill parents, new neighbors, a stolen car, and a kid's school awards. By the time he got back to the gate the people were chatting among themselves. The prospect of a riot had been totally defused with not a police club lifted or a person arrested.

Asked later why his approach had worked, Officer Weinberg said that when the crowd was thinking of rioting, they were thinking only of the excitement, not of the possible consequences. When he reminded the leaders of their individual concerns, they started to think more clearly about the down side of mass violence.

Let's talk about a variety of law-enforcement situations in which you might find yourself confronted by the police when other people are involved or the circumstances are unusual. Although the basic recommendations about confrontations still apply, there are additional concerns in each of these cases.

Case One: Participating in a Demonstration

Many people participate in demonstrations to show their support of, or objection to, some issue. They demonstrate in front of stores and public buildings, at meetings, and even at people's homes.

However, every community has laws to regulate peaceful demonstrations. Smart people do not join a demonstration until they find out whether the leaders know the regulations and intend to follow them.

In most cases, demonstrators need a police permit. The permit usually specifies starting and ending times, where participants can stand, and how many people can take part.

If you are in charge of a demonstration, start by calling the police and asking whether a permit is needed from them or from the city or county government. Permits also give the police time to plan how to regulate traffic flow around the event, provide staff to protect the demonstrators, and in some cases arrange for first-aid equipment to be on the scene. For example, on an extremely hot day demonstrators might suffer heat stroke and need an ambulance.

A peaceful demonstration is just that. People may dance, yell, talk through bullhorns (unless there is a sound ordinance), and wave banners with slogans. As long as everyone respects the rights of others, the demonstration is considered peaceful.

However, if the police believe that violence might break out, they have the right to ask the demonstrators to disperse; that is, to scatter and leave the area. If you are asked to disperse, it is best to move on. If the demonstrators refuse to do so, the police have the right to use as much force as is needed to break up the group.

How to Avoid Being Arrested

In general, the police will simply watch a peaceful group. They may wear riot gear to remind the crowd to behave itself, but they rarely try to interact with the demonstrators.

If you see that a demonstration is getting out of control, move to the fringe of the crowd, as far away from the police as possible. You can continue to express your feelings there, but if the crowd turns wild, you are more likely to get away safely.

When a Demonstration Gets Out of Hand

Under most conditions, people respect a police officer's badge and what it stands for. As people leave a ballgame, for example, a single officer may stand at the gate directing traffic. In reality, he is no match for the five or six hundred cars driving toward him, but because people respect his job they turn according to his commands.

But sometimes, a group of people turns into a mob and starts to riot. This is dangerous because the ordinary patrol officer is helpless under such conditions. The people override the meaning of the badge and turn into a mob that no longer respects authority. That's the definition of a riot.

It's a Riot!

When a riot begins, police call for the riot squad. The situation has become the equivalent of a small war. The riot police come in battle dress, may use armored cars, and have a large array of weapons.

Your smartest move is being away from the center of the mob. There you are least likely to get hurt or to be arrested. The police often try to arrest the leaders in the center of the action first, since the leaders often control the flow of the demonstration.

If you have friends with you, don't talk among yourselves about what to do. Quickly move first, and then call your friends over to you. If you cannot get away from the action, protect yourself as well as you can. The police are likely to arrest anyone they can get their hands on, especially anyone they see fighting or looting. Don't take anything that does not belong to you.

Television cameras and camcorders are frequently trained on riot scenes. If cameras show up, don't try to get in the picture. You may regret the impulse to say, "Hi, Mom!" or to wave to your friends. Police often check pictures and use them as evidence to support an arrest.

Protect Your Personal Safety

If people in the crowd or members of the police become angry and violent, try to take any blows on your back or shoulders. Cover your head with your arms, books, or backpack as you run.

Because the police are supposed to use guns or clubs as little as possible, they use a variety of nonlethal ways to control crowds. Tear gas or pepper spray are often used. Wherever you are, try to get away from where a gas canister lands. If you are out in the open, move in the direction from which the wind is blowing. Wind blows the gases quickly.

If you can, cover your nose and eyes with a wet cloth— a towel, your T-shirt, your shirttail, a wet tissue. Some veterans of demonstrations actually carry a damp cloth in a plastic bag to be prepared if the demonstration gets out of hand.

If hit by tear gas or mace, wash your eyes and face with cold water, as quickly as you can. Wash repeatedly until the stinging stops.

Not Friendly Fido

Often the police bring their trained dogs along. If a dog runs toward you, stand perfectly still and make no effort to be friendly. Don't stare the dog in the eye because the dog sees that as a hostile act. If you are knocked down, cover your head and face with your arms and lie perfectly still. The dog is highly trained and is not likely to bite you unless you act aggressively toward him or his handler. If you are holding a stick or anything that might be used as a weapon, toss it away before the dog gets near you.

How to Be Arrested Safely

If the police are determined to arrest you, and you are determined to be arrested, do not fight the police. The safest thing is to offer to go quietly. Ask the officer what he or she wants you to do.

Some demonstrators who are seeking publicity "go limp" when arrested by relaxing their bodies completely. The police may not be pleased if you do so, but they will probably treat you better than if you struggle or abuse them verbally.

Is Breaking a Law Worth the Price?

Suppose you feel so concerned about a cause that you don't want to leave when the police tell you that you must.

If you stay on, you are risking arrest. Be sure you seriously believe that the cause is worth the price of your being arrested and possibly going to jail for a short time. If you are arrested and convicted, you will have to report that fact on every job application for the rest of your life, unless you are a minor. Many years down the road, this arrest might keep you from getting a job you want very much. Only you can decide whether you're willing to take that risk.

Case Two: Joining a Strike

A strike is a type of demonstration. You and your fellow workers want to protest working conditions that you think are unfair, so you picket your company. Usually strikes are peaceful, but they can also turn into a mob scene. Be prepared.

If some workers (called "scabs") try to cross your picket line to take over the jobs of those on strike, you can ask them to respect the strike. Don't try to detain them forcibly or assault them. The use of physical force is grounds for arrest. Getting arrested does not do your cause any good. The ever-present camera or camcorder will probably make you look like the aggressor on the TV news.

Crossing a Picket Line

On the other hand, suppose you do not support a strike and you decide to cross a picket line. Read the body language of the people on the picket line. Try to cross it where there is someone who does not look very angry. If a man is yelling obscenities and waving a banner on a heavy stick, cross elsewhere. Look for someone who is standing quietly and does not appear to threaten people. Move quietly, quickly, and with no verbal exchange. Go into the building as quickly as you can. If someone takes a swing at you, duck and keep moving. Do not respond to swear words or other verbal attacks.

At the end of the day, go out the same way you went in. Find a quiet place to cross the line and move quickly and decisively, with no smart remarks.

Case Three: Spring Break

Spring break fever is a madness that many young adults experience for a week or two around March or April. Thousands of people in their teens and early twenties leap into cars and head for beaches and recreation areas.

In many resort communities, the city leaders gear up for the invasion. They hire extra police; work with motels, restaurants, and other businesses to set reasonable guidelines for behavior; and look forward to the extra money that will come into the community. Sometimes, however, the community is unprepared and the police are less than tolerant of the visitors.

Most of the recreation resorts relax their rules a bit for the occasion, but you need to find out the rules in the area. If the community you plan to visit is tough on young people and you don't want to put up with the restrictions, don't go there.

At some beaches and resorts, the police pay little attention to underage drinking as long as the young people don't flaunt it and don't become violent. At others, they stay alert for underage drinking and arrest anyone who is found guilty. Fake ID cards are checked and confiscated.

Officer J. Evans of Crescent Beach, Florida, reminds young people that Crescent Beach is his home and that he expects visitors to treat the area the way they would treat their own town. He also points out that many beaches are governed by the same laws as public roads. You can drive on some beaches and not on others. You need to know the local laws governing beaches before using them.

On spring break you want to have a good time without dealing with the police at all. You don't want to need their help or be arrested. Take measures to avoid ever needing police help. Protect your money by carrying only a single credit card, no checkbook, and limited cash. Sleep with the card on your person, and let no one use it. Even good friends may "borrow" cash but fail to pay it back, or use your credit card "just this one time" and run up staggering bills. Promises are not always kept, and you are responsible for charges to a credit card unless you can prove theft.

The police will try to help you if money is stolen from you by a mugger or pickpocket, but they can do little to recover stolen goods in a town filled with young people who are there for only a few days. They will offer you little or no help for money you lose to friends or through carelessness. That isn't their job.

Carla, only sixteen, was delighted when a bunch of senior girls in her high school invited her to go to the beach with them. Her reluctant parents let her go when she promised to "be good." The partying turned wild by the second day. Drug and alcohol odors filled their hotel room. A young man befriended Carla, and she invited him to join the gang sleeping in her room. She felt that life couldn't get any more exciting.

By the third day, the other girls groaned that they had spent all their money and began begging Carla for some of her large allowance. Proud to be able to help her friends, she kept lending money until she was almost broke. That night the whole bunch, including Carla, went cruising. Looking for a place to buy more beer, they soon became lost in a town near where they were staying.

When the siren suddenly sounded behind them, the driver of the car admitted to the others that she was going the wrong way on a one-way street, but had thought it might be a shortcut to the liquor store.

There was no way to get rid of the beer bottles or the papers and the stashes, so the girls tried to sit on them. The officer looked inside the car and noticed the awkward position of the four girls crammed into the back seat. He ordered everyone out of the car. Moments later they were all under arrest.

At the station house, the officers asked each girl to empty her pockets and purse. Carla soon saw that her friends, who had proclaimed to be "broke," produced great stacks of money. It poured from wallets. It rolled out from fanny packs. One girl had $50 hidden in her underwear. Suddenly Carla realized why she had been invited to go along with them on spring break. It was a bitter lesson.

Staying Away from the Police

Going along with your friends is okay most of the time, but not when it includes breaking a law. Police do not care why you are involved in an illegal act. They look at the facts as they see them. If you go along for the midnight raid on the hot dog stand, you will stand trial with the rest.

Only you can make up your mind to enjoy spring break without having to pay physically, emotionally, or financially. Trashing a motel room and having to pay for all the damage or being arrested for hurting someone while in a drunken rage can be some of the awful results of a careless spring break. Take a spring break, but don't end up broke, blasted, or busted.

Case Four: Gangs

Of all the special cases, gangs pose the most difficult problem. Almost everyone likes to have a sense of belonging to a particular group: family, religious, social, athletic, and so on. Most of us have such group affiliations, and they add to the quality of our lives. We say, "I am a New York Yankees fan," or "I am a Baptist." By belonging, we get personal satisfaction, and we follow the general rules of the group. The rules of most groups do not break any laws or encourage confrontations with the police.

A gang, however, often bands together to protect its turf and members. In doing so, the gang often violates public laws, and the members are told to follow gang rules instead of the established laws. Almost always, membership in a gang automatically means an increase in confrontations with the police.

The smart answer is to avoid joining the gang. Once you are in, you'll have a tough time breaking away. Police will identify you as a gang member and watch you closely in malls, on the street, or in your car.

Do not make friends with known gang members or hang out with the gang. Instead, look for social groups and friends outside a gang.

But what if you belong to a gang now? You already know about police confrontations. If you want to live a more peaceful life, find out if others have ever left your gang successfully and how they did it. In time, you may be able to do the same. Meanwhile, try to move to the fringe of the gang. Don't be the one to lead in confrontations with the police. Obey the civil laws of your community whenever you can. When you do have police confrontations, follow the suggestions in this book. No matter what laws you have broken, you still have certain civil rights.

Case Five: When Your Minority Group Seems Targeted by the Police

Let's suppose you have had a stressful encounter with the police. You believe you were stopped because of your color. Even so, you kept your temper and your tongue under control. You realize that there is no way to prove you were in the right. You feel powerless. But you are not powerless. You can do a lot to help yourself and your community.

First, help yourself. Get rid of some of the stress caused by the incident by playing a hard game of ball or running around the gym fifty times or punching a pillow until you are exhausted. Bottled-up stress will not change the situation, but it can do your body damage. Moreover, the next time you encounter the police and you have not dealt with your anger, you may turn it loose even though it may not be appropriate.

Second, direct your anger toward joining with others to force an improvement in police/community relations. Talk to leaders in your churches, local government, and news media about the problem. If well-respected people in these groups agree that change is needed, talk about what actions can be taken. Join a political-action group that can work with you to take effective action. Many communities have made significant changes in the quality of police work once the issues have been brought to public attention.

Case Six: Traveling in Foreign Countries

If you travel to another country, be sure to learn something about the laws of the country and the nature of the police before you go. This includes Canada and Mexico; for example, carrying a firearm into Mexico is against the law even if you have a U.S. permit. Although the U.S. imprisons far more people than other civilized countries, most other countries have quicker, harsher punishments. Drug arrests in many countries are very serious. Even possession of a small amount of drugs can get you life imprisonment. Obey the law, even if you notice that the locals do not.

Should you for any reason, guilty or innocent, be arrested in a foreign country, ask at once to make contact with the American Embassy. Often the Embassy can intervene on your behalf.

If you go abroad, use your head. Don't let friends, television, or movies give you ideas about how to behave. If you don't know whether something is okay to do, find out. Or don't do it at all!

Tips for Getting Help and Preventing Crime

I n real life, police are mostly good guys. The majority of the police really do work hard at living up to the obligations of their badges. If it weren't for the police, who would stop the speeders on our street? Or face up to the angry man who is shooting randomly in the fast-food restaurant? Or enter a dark alley to catch a rapist?

9-1-1 is still the most used number in the phone book. No matter what we feel about the police, when an emergency arises, we can call 9-1-1 and expect to get help.

What Is 9-1-1?

Nearly every community has a 9-1-1 emergency telephone number. Cellular phones often use a different number, such as #77, to report highway emergencies. Signs along the highways and interstates tell you what number to use to call the police or an ambulance.

In most places, 9-1-1 connects you with a central office that handles all police, fire, and rescue calls. Several people sit at a room-sized switchboard and take the calls. In the most up-to-date centers, everything is handled by a sophisticated computer. When a call comes in, the number of the telephone being used is shown on a screen, along with the name and address of the person whose telephone is being used to make the call.

As soon as you are connected, the operator will ask you whether you want police, fire, or rescue. Why are these services combined? Many times two or more of the services are needed in an emergency. If a car in a wreck bursts into flames and some of the occupants are injured, police, fire, and rescue are all needed at the scene.

Hans looked out the window of his new apartment and stared at the street. He was already homesick for Germany. As he looked, two cars came flying around the corner. The second car deliberately sped up, sideswiped the first car into a lamppost, and sped away. Hans could hear the metal crunch. He grabbed his phone and hit the 9-1-1 keys the apartment manager had told him would get help.

A voice said, "Police, fire, or rescue?"

His English was not good. He fought for the right words.

"Just one minute," the voice said. Suddenly another voice got on the line, speaking with a familiar German accent.

The next day Hans read in the local paper that quick action by an onlooker had helped paramedics save the life of someone in the car that was hit. He also read that the police had arrested the drunken driver of the other car.

Today, with the advantages of computers, the 9-1-1 services are increasingly able to help everyone. People who are deaf or hard of hearing may call in on their text telephone (TTY). If you speak a language other than English, many systems now switch your call to a central number in California, where people can interpret just about any language. They relay the information in English to your local operator.

Using an Emergency Number

In an emergency, speak clearly and slowly. Here are some points to keep in mind:

1. Start by stating the main problem. For example:
   "Police. Someone is in my house!"
   "Fire. My house is on fire!" (Remember, first get everyone out of the house. Always call from another telephone if your house is on fire.)
   "Rescue. My mom just fainted. Send an ambulance."

2. Next, identify yourself. For example:
   "I'm Jenny Jacobs and I'm at 131 Main Street. My phone number is 555-1213."

3. Briefly explain the situation. For example:
   If you are alone, say so.
   If there are special conditions, such as a person in a wheelchair or a baby in a crib, say so, especially in case of a fire or hostage situation.

4. Stay on the line if you possibly can while the operator asks additional questions. As we said, the

operator will have a printout only of the number and address from which you are calling. Make it clear right away if you are not calling from the site of the emergency.

After you hang up, the operator often calls back to be sure the call was not a prank. Answer the phone and confirm your request.

Once an operator has the needed information, he or she will dispatch equipment and personnel as quickly as possible. Often, help is on the way while you are still answering questions.

When *Not* to Call 9-1-1

Don't dial 9-1-1 *unless you have an emergency*. The operator at the central office must handle all calls as if they are emergencies. By emergency, the police mean a situation in which the speed of response will make a difference either in your safety or in catching a criminal. Tying up a squad car for a matter that could wait for an hour or even a day or two may take the police away from a true emergency. If you come home from vacation and find that someone has spattered paint on your house, you do not have an emergency.

For routine problems, use the telephone number for the police station nearest you. You can find that number in your telephone book, or call information. Find what that number is and write it down before you need it.

You should use that number instead of 9-1-1 for such concerns as:

• Checking when the town meeting on crime prevention is going to be held.

- Reporting the need for a traffic light at your corner.
- Complaining that more and more speeders are using your street as a shortcut.

If you call 9-1-1 frequently for small things, the operators will get to know your name. Then if something awful does happen to you, they may think you are making another unimportant call and not take you seriously.

Never make a false 9-1-1 call. Making such calls is against the law. You may prevent someone who has a real emergency from being helped.

Help the Police to Help You

Before you have a life or death matter, there are things you can do to help the police (or fire or ambulance crews) to help you.

- Your house or apartment should have clearly written numbers that are big enough to be seen. If it doesn't, and you don't own the building, print the number of the building and your apartment number in *big* letters on cardboard and put the sign in a window facing the street.
- Have your street address, apartment number, and phone number written down next to every telephone. If you are excited when you call, you might say you live at 532 Main Street instead of 523. If a visitor makes the call for you, he or she may not know the information.

Why the Police Can't Always Come Right Away

Although the police try to respond to calls immediately, they often have too few officers to handle every call as soon as it comes in. They try to give priority to calls that involve a life-threatening situation.

Suppose you see some teens breaking into a car. You call 9-1-1, but the police don't come right away and the teens escape with the car. The police may be trying to help someone who has a burglar in her house. A problem that threatens someone's safety has to have their full attention before they can get to work on a case involving personal property.

Some people say that when they reported that someone had stolen their television set, the police all but yawned. They wondered why the police didn't get more upset and do something more quickly.

The police are rarely as upset as the public about small crimes, especially theft or damage to property. These crimes often get less attention than the public would like because the chances the police will catch the culprit are not great, and because crimes involving people get priority.

The theft of your television set may be the most upsetting thing that has happened to your family all year, but it also may be the twentieth burglary the police have handled that week. From their point of view, the burglar didn't get much compared to the $100,000 bank robbery earlier in the day.

Yes, you pay the police their salaries. Yes, you have a right to get help from them. But, no, you will not always come first, nor can you expect them to be as upset about what happened as you are.

When *Not* to Call the Police

Do not ask the police to help solve a problem if some other person or group is supposed to do the job.

The policeman who helped to open a pickle jar (remember him?) had the time to help, but usually they don't.

When you have a problem, check the front pages or blue pages of your telephone book for community support groups/agencies, or call the information office of your city or county to find out who is supposed to handle such problems. For example, police are not supposed to clear snow from the front of the post office even though people are falling down. Don't call the police. Call the main post office in your town.

Auto Accidents

Most states have laws about what to do when you have an auto accident. Unless it is only a minor fender-bender, have someone call the police and an ambulance, if one is needed.

Don't leave the scene until the police come. If you were in any way involved, you must stay there no matter how important it is for you to be somewhere else.

Try to see that any cars involved are pulled off on the side of the road, if possible, and engines turned off. If someone seems to have a neck or back injury, move them as little as possible. Most states have "good Samaritan laws," which protect you from being sued for trying to help someone who is injured.

As the police are collecting information, you should also record the names, home and work phone numbers, and insurance company names/numbers of all those involved in the accident. Jot down the license plate numbers of all cars involved. Also write down names and phone numbers of any witnesses who will identify themselves.

A "Car Accident Information" form is printed in the back of this book. Photocopy it, and keep copies in the glove compartment of the car or cars you drive.

If You Are a Victim of Crime

Sadly, some of us are going to be victims of crimes. You, or someone you care about, may be mugged or beaten or sexually attacked. If any of these things happen, call the police and let them deal with the offender. Do not take matters into your own hands, no matter how angry you are. More than one person has shot a suspect, believing they had the right to do so, only to find themselves on trial for their actions. You have the right only to protect yourself and shoot in self-defense.

Rape and Sexual Assault

"Do you like Dave?" Liz's best friend Megan asked.
"Oh, yes!"

Liz glowed at the thought of her first date with Dave. True, he had come on strong and tried to talk her into sex, even though they hardly knew each other. "You know you want to," he had said several times.

They saw each other again. Again he pressured her to have sex with him. She liked Dave a lot, but why was he rushing her? He was so relentless in his pursuit for sex that she felt uneasy. She couldn't explain it—even to Megan.

After a party that Saturday, Liz went to Dave's house. It was late but she was having fun. Suddenly, he turned on her and forced her to have sex with him.

Afterwards, when he went to the bathroom for a minute, she dressed quickly and hurried home. What should she do? After all, he was no stranger.

Should she:

- Report to the police she had been raped?
- Talk to her parents?
- Talk to Megan?
- Talk to someone at her church?
- See her doctor?

Whether male or female, if you have been raped or sexually assaulted, try to report the incident to the police, and try to do it as soon as possible. The person who hurt you is a criminal. You did not deserve to have the assault happen.

If you choose to report the incident don't bathe or change clothes beforehand. Be aware you will have to answer questions and re-live the event while you may be in shock. All of this may be difficult, but that is the only way the police can gather evidence that will hold up in court if they arrest the offender. In the best of communities, you will be examined by a doctor or nurse and evidence will be taken of body fluids, hairs, or blood on your clothing.

Sadly, in some places, reporting a rape or sexual assault is still a bad experience. If you have been known to have an active sex life, the police may not respond well to your complaint. If you have been drinking alcohol, many police may not consider a sexual assault to be rape and may dissuade you from pressing charges. If so, locate a women's support group or organization in your community that helps survivors of rape or sexual assault. Staff or trained volunteers can discuss what happened and what your legal options are, or they can refer you to another agency that offers help they do not.

Then, check with your nearest health clinic or family doctor if you want medical and/or psychological support. Don't be embarrassed to ask for assistance if you need it— you didn't do anything to deserve being victimized.

Protecting Your Home

The police are glad to help you keep from needing their help. For example, some homes almost invite burglars. Many cities or counties have specially trained officers who tour homes, point out spots that would attract a burglar, and suggest ways to make the home look less inviting to an intruder. They can tell you what to do to make a burglar think "Why bother?" and go away. You'll be saved the anguish of losing things you value, and the police will be saved the work of filling out a report and trying to find the burglar.

Protecting Yourself

Below is an A-B-C-D-E checklist of things you can do to protect yourself. How many of them are you careful about?

- *Avoid going out alone at night in areas where crimes often occur.* If you have to go out, go in pairs or a group. If you will be driving in a strange area, check out your route before you go. Carry a map and a flashlight with you.
- *Be alert.* Watch what is going on around you. Don't just walk to your car through a parking lot at night.

Look around. Are you alone? Is someone standing near your car? Take a quick look inside. Is someone lying down on the back seat? Don't give car-jackers an edge.

- *Check out laws that apply to you and your family.* Did you know that in some states a child must be at least eight years old (or, in some areas, older) to be left alone? Or that in many states a person must be thirteen to baby-sit legally? Such laws may seem severe to a capable youngster, but they have become needed as our society becomes more dangerous.

- *Don't be alone in an elevator with a suspicious-looking person.* Listen to your instincts. Better to be safe and embarrass yourself or someone else than to be sorry. Our instincts often give us good warnings about dangerous people and situations. Just not being there is sometimes the best form of self-defense.

- *Escape with your life.* If, despite being careful, you are approached by a criminal in a public place, your best bet is to yell and run. Few criminals will shoot under those conditions. If you are alone and in an unprotected place, don't fight a mugger's demands. Give up your money, your coat, your shoes, your bike, or your jewelry—not your life.

When Criminals Pose As Police

Females should be especially aware of the increase in crimes against women by men posing as police. If the officer is in an unmarked car, look closely at his uniform and ID. At night, unmarked cars are seldom used by the actual police. Barbara Childress, Chief of Police in Richland

Hills, Texas, recommends the following if you are driving in a car and are asked to pull over by a supposed police officer:

- Keep driving with emergency flashers on until you reach a well-lighted area with other people around.
- Lead the way to an area of your own choosing. Do not follow the unidentified car to an area of their choosing.
- When you stop, keep doors locked and the engine running. Open the window only enough to ask the officer for his or her identification.
- If you are still uncertain, ask that a supervisor be summoned.

While an officer may get upset or frustrated with your request, it's important to insist if you firmly believe your safety is at stake.

Community Policing

Recently, many police chiefs have started pushing the concept of community policing. They insist that the officers get out of their cars and walk the streets so they will get to know the people they serve. In other places, the officers are put on bikes or horseback. The idea is that officers who know people as individuals are less likely to be ruled by racial or other bias in dealing with them and will be so visible that criminals will hesitate to act.

Police researchers also believe that people who know and trust an officer are more likely to work with the police to help prevent and solve crimes.

When Anne agreed to go fishing with her brother, she never dreamed what a big fish they would catch.

Their favorite fishing spot was located in an area a mile from the nearest road. Carrying their gear, Anne and Carl hiked the old fishing trail along Seneca Creek. About halfway to the spot, Anne saw a plume of smoke drifting down the stream on the breeze.

"There's not supposed to be any fires in here today," she said to Carl. "Let's go back and call Ranger McKay to come check this out."

"We don't have to go back," said Carl, pulling his cellular phone out of his pack and dialing the ranger station.

"Stay right where you are. Don't investigate," said McKay when he answered. "That fire may come from the firebug who has been causing us big trouble. He may be dangerous."

Although it seemed a long wait to Carl and Anne, McKay and two other armed, uniformed rangers arrived quickly. Telling Carl and Anne to stay put, the two men and the woman slipped quietly up the nearby slope and circled above the source of the fire. Suddenly they moved down on the firebug with drawn guns. The struggle was over almost before it began.

Moments later, the rangers walked back along the trail with a handcuffed man in tow.

"Thanks a lot," said McKay to Anne and Carl. "This is a character we've been trying to catch for some time. He won't be setting any more fires in this place. Good luck with your fishing."

The man scowled at Anne and Carl, but they ignored him and headed to their fishing hole, pleased with themselves for having helped protect their favorite park.

As another part of community outreach, police departments support a variety of activities, such as the DARE drug-prevention program in schools. They also sponsor dances, ball teams, and youth clubs. These are all ways for officers to get to know the people they serve and to prevent crime by offering young people and adults safe and enjoyable ways to spend their leisure time.

Ride-Along Programs

Another popular program lets citizens learn about the police department firsthand. In ride-along programs, citizens actually ride with the police on calls. Check the police department nearest you and ask if they have such a program.

You will never forget a ride-along trip. It will give you some idea of the courage and intelligence it takes to be a really good police officer.

If you can't get a ride-along trip, ask whether tours of the department are available so that you can learn more about the inside work of the police. One thing you will see at a station house is the great amount of records that police must keep. You'll see why in Chapter 10 we urge you to keep your own records of any police encounter!

Get to Know the Police on Your Own

If there is no program in your town for getting to know the police, don't let that stop you. Get to know the police on your own. Walk up to the officer on your street, smile, and say something like this: "Hello. My name is Tony. What's it like being a police officer in this place?"

If he or she says something like, "Why do you want to know?", you can answer, "I don't know much about police work, and I thought you might tell me a little." If that officer won't talk, say, "Thanks, anyway," and walk away. Try again with another officer. Most officers will be glad to talk with you if they have the time. Of course, use good sense. Don't flag down a patrol car and ask the driver to talk. Instead, talk to an officer standing on the street or one who is having a cup of coffee.

Talking to an officer is something you should do only when you are alone. If you try to do it with a bunch of friends, a suspicious officer may think you are up to no good.

Getting to know the police in your community probably won't keep you from getting a ticket the next time you're caught speeding. But you may understand them better, and that understanding may help you cope better with the police during your next encounter.

CHAPTER ◇ 9

Private Police

The year is 1968. The want ads target off-duty police who would like to be hired for a weekend with good pay. The hundreds who show up for the interview are told they are to work a three-day outdoor concert involving perhaps hundreds of thousands of people—but they cannot carry any weapons!

Hearing that, many turn away.

Those who remain are told that they will not wear regular uniforms either. They'll wear bell-bottom jeans and fire-engine red shirts with peace symbols on them. Their job is to keep the peace, not enforce the law.

Many more walk away.

The remaining group, under the leadership of police administrator Wesley Pomeroy, became the famous "non-cops" of the Woodstock Festival—arguably one of the most peaceful privately policed outdoor concerts ever.

Around the world, people have long hired others to protect them, their businesses, their homes, and their possessions. Sharpshooters rode shotgun on carriages and stagecoaches to protect people and goods. "Bulls" kept hobos off trains and caught train robbers. Today, floorwalkers watch for shoplifters in stores. Night watch-men guard warehouses after dark. Bodyguards protect people from stalkers and enemies. Guards control entry into mansions and other buildings where the famous, the wealthy, or the politically important work or live.

Today, over a million people are privately employed to keep the peace, protect an area, person, or product, and sometimes enforce the law. You are so used to seeing them that you may not be aware of them. But from the guard at the museum to the receptionist at the medical building to the plainclothes store detective, private law enforcers play a part in our lives.

Depending on where they work and what their job involves, these private law enforcers have various names:

- Asset protector
- Loss prevention employee
- Bodyguard
- Store detective
- Security guard
- Private eye
- Night watchman
- Rent-a-Cop

No matter what their title, these persons differ from the civil police because their power does not come from the public. They do not represent you and me. The private police, in most instances, get their limited power from their employer—a store, a mall, a concert center, an airport, a famous person, or a private firm or agency.

Private police are sometimes hired by governments to support the services of the local, state, and federal police. They help deter crime by giving the appearance that an area has more police than it actually does.

Because they do not have the power of civil police, few private police need the background or training of law officers. Private detectives and guards who work for agencies like Pinkerton Security Services and Wells, Fargo Alarm Services are governed by laws that specify what training they must have and what they can and cannot do. For most private police, however, the education and experience required depends on the specific work they are expected to do. Their training is on the job.

The Job of Private Police

The primary job of private police is to do what the employer asks of them. Guards who work for Pinkerton and Wells, Fargo continue their historic role of protecting shipments of money and property. Private detectives often carry out such time-consuming tasks as investigating insurance claims, finding runaways, and checking on cheating spouses.

Government-hired private police do a variety of tasks. Their roles are very different from those of the civil police. They may tow illegally parked cars, control traffic, patrol parking meters, fingerprint prisoners, and guard public buildings such as a sports arena and the town hall.

The private police you are most likely to encounter are those in malls, stores, and offices. They primarily fill two major roles: helping the public, and keeping the peace.

Despite their uniforms, they are hired mainly to answer questions, direct clients and customers, and generally discourage trouble. Some do work undercover, but most carry out their jobs by being obvious.

Although they are not fully empowered police, they have enough power to cause you problems if you come in conflict with them.

Two young African American men went into Flawntie's, an upscale specialty store. One of the youths was
stopped by the store detective and asked if he was
wearing a Flawntie shirt. When the young man said
yes, the detective asked him to produce a receipt for
the shirt. The young man did not have it with him,
since he had bought the shirt the week before. He
explained that his friend had liked the shirt so well
that they had come to buy him one like it. The store
detective ordered the young man to take off the
shirt and leave it at the store until he produced the
receipt. The young man protested, but finally
complied. Shirtless, he left the store, much embarrassed at having to remove clothing in public. Later
he returned with the receipt and retrieved his
shirt.

The following day, he called the head office of the
Flawntie company and also told the news media what
had happened. The Flawntie company apologized
and tried to make amends to the young man. As a
public relations gesture, they contributed clothing to
the poor. But a lawsuit brought by the family is now
pending.

Getting Along with Private Police

In dealing with private police in malls or anywhere else,
follow the guidelines for dealing with police confrontations if you are stopped (see Chapter 5). If you trigger
trouble by using obscene gestures or curse words, or even
actual violence, the private police person may use force
in self-defense. Don't give anyone an opportunity to
become violent toward you.

In interviews, a number of mall guards told us that they feel little need to be concerned when they see a young person who comes alone or with a family to shop. When two young people come into the mall together, the guards become uneasy. When a group of young people come together, the guards prepare for what they expect to be trouble. You may or may not agree with their attitude. Nevertheless, it suggests that if you really need to shop for that just-right pair of jeans, you might want to either go alone or with only one friend. If you do decide to go to the mall with a few friends, be aware of the guards' point of view. Don't act loud or rowdy if you want to avoid trouble.

If any major problem occurs, most privately hired police use back-up assistance from police officers, who handle any arrests or charges. The private police merely detain a person they suspect of breaking the law.

Three male juveniles went into a major department store. The store guard saw each of them shoplifting and stopped them as they tried to leave the store. Instead of cooperating, one of them kicked the guard in the shins and all of them started running. The guard, a former high school athlete, set out in pursuit and caught two of them. Twisting their arms behind their backs, he walked them back to the store.

Meanwhile, the store manager had called the police. When they arrived, the two pointed out the third one, who was driving a car around the parking lot looking for them.

The police arrested the third youth and confiscated the car as well, because it contained beer and drugs and had no license plate. The three were charged with possession of drugs and alcohol, and stealing. The driver was also charged with driving without proper plates.

The boys underestimated the authority of the mall guards and ended up paying a big price for their ignorance and lack of respect.

Your Rights in Dealing with Private Police

You do have rights in dealing with private police, whether you're guilty or innocent of causing trouble.

Sarah and Elizabeth decided they needed new outfits for a class picnic. Both had empty wallets and parents who firmly said, "No more money this month." Hmm, what to do? Shoplift! Why not? They were as clever and smart as friends who had done it.

As a clerk rang up a sale for someone else, they each put a pair of shorts into bags that held socks they had paid for. They didn't realize that the shopper across the aisle was an undercover security worker for the store. They laughed at how clever they had been as they walked casually through the mall.

Three steps outside the mall they were stopped by an officer. He was dressed in an official-looking uniform and wore a badge. "Please come with me," he said firmly.

With the goods on them, the girls admitted that they had stolen the shorts. They were fingerprinted and had their pictures taken, and were ordered not to enter the mall for the next year. Both girls felt foolish and not a bit clever as they waited for their parents to pick them up and take them home.

Later, the girls realized that their rights had not been read to them. What should they and their families do?

- Go to court to fight their punishment because they were not read their rights?
- Figure that they got off easy and put the incident behind them?
- Write a letter of complaint to the police department with copies to the mayor and the local newspaper?
- Read this book to understand why their rights weren't read?

Private police will no doubt question you as soon as you are detained. Even if you know the civil police are on the way, you have the right not to say anything that will incriminate you. You will not be read your rights until and unless you are turned over to the civil police and they decide there are sufficient grounds for an arrest.

You should know that store managers often ban for life anyone who is caught changing price tags or shoplifting. That means the shoplifter can never enter that store again for any reason.

Cop or Non-Cop?

Here's important information: Many police officers earn extra money on their time off as private law enforcers. If they see someone commit a crime, big or small, they can revert to their role as police officers and make arrests.

So how can you know if you are dealing with private police or civil police? There is no sure way to know. The sensible thing is to treat all uniformed persons with appropriate courtesy. Even the doorman at a hotel might be an undercover cop!

Watch Out!

Not only do you often not know whether you are dealing with a civil officer or a private policeperson, you often have no way of knowing what electronic devices are used to watch you. Nearly all private police, as well as civil police, today rely on mechanical gadgets of various types to back up their observations. Many stores have security cameras that operate twenty-four hours a day. Stores that sell clothing attach detectors to expensive items. The detectors sound an alarm if you try to take the clothes without paying for them. Some stores deactivate unseen detectors when they scan the product as you buy it. If you have flown from a major airport or entered a secured building, you have had the experience of walking through a metal detector. And video cameras are everywhere.

But cameras are not always sure proof of guilt. Much depends on the camera angle and the quality of the picture as to what a later viewer of the film sees. Machines, whether electronic or not, aren't any better than the person who installs them, uses them, and knows when they do not operate correctly. Anyone who has ever worked with a machine, whether a camcorder, a computer, or a car, knows that machines can and do malfunction. Increasing numbers of us may find ourselves charged with a crime we didn't commit.

Accused by Mistake

What should you do if you are falsely accused? The best answer is an honest denial and lots of patience. Don't panic. Don't fight anyone physically or yell threats or curses. Eventually, with time and a cool attitude matters should be straightened out.

Len had wanted to go to a Nine Inch Nails concert for months. They were his favorite group. He heard they were soon to play at the local sports arena.

Len was second in line the morning the tickets went on sale, and he bought tickets for himself and his best friend. The night of the show they arrived early and found places right in front of the stage.

The show was everything Len had hoped: the music was loud and the crowd was wild—maybe a little too wild.

The electrical system suddenly broke down and all the amps stopped blasting. The crowd cheered at first; as stage hands kept working and nothing happened, the crowd got restless. Someone threw a folding chair. Then another. A riot seemed ready to break out.

"Let's get out of here," said Len. He looked around and saw that the steps leading backstage were still clear. The two of them raced up the steps—and right into the arms of a guard.

"All right, you two. We heard some of you were gonna crash this group backstage. Just come along quietly and I won't hurt you."

But he did hurt them. He twisted their arms up behind their heads. The more they tried to explain why they were backstage, the tighter and more painful his hold became. A few minutes later they found themselves flung on the ground in a back alley. The rest of the concert they heard from a distance as they walked to their car.

The next day, Len told his dad what had happened.

"Why don't you write to the management?" his dad suggested.

Len did just that. He wrote a careful account of

what had happened and described the guard. He asked the management either to refund his money or give him tickets to the next concert.

A week later Len got a note with apologies from the manager of the arena and a statement that the guard would be reprimanded. Two gift certificates for tickets to future concerts were enclosed.

You do not need to let a mall guard or concert guard hassle you. If you're minding your own business and not causing trouble, you do not have to leave the premises unless you are trespassing.

If a private police officer hurts you or wrongfully accuses you, and there is nothing you can do about it at the time, your best bet is to write a complete report of what happened. Use the information in the next chapter about SNAP reports to make your report as accurate as possible.

In most cases, the management that has hired the private law enforcer wants your business. If you are at the mall, they want you to come back and buy often in those stores. If you are at a concert, the management wants you to enjoy it and buy a ticket the next time. The success of their business depends on creating good feelings with their customers.

Suppose a concert guard treats you the way Len and his friend were treated. Write a report as soon as possible after the incident. The first place to leave a copy of the report is at the management office of the person who hired the security officer. If a manager wants to talk to you, be prepared to answer the following questions: Do you simply want an apology? Do you want the guard fired? Do you plan to bring suit?

Suing costs a lot of money and is not practical unless you have a very strong case. Only a lawyer can tell you that. The best you may get is an apology.

If the situation was very embarrassing, as in the case of the young man at the Flawntie store, consider alerting the media. If you and your family are up to the publicity, the local newspaper and TV station would probably be interested in a copy of your report.

Whether an incident involved a police officer or a private law enforcer, a report can help you in any situation that grows out of an encounter or confrontation. Let's talk about how to prepare a report.

CHAPTER 10

Reporting a Confrontation

One night your family's car is stolen from your driveway. Your parents report the loss to the police department. Two days later, a family friend calls. "Guess what," she says. "I'm sure it's your car sitting in the parking lot behind Moneta Mall." After finding the car, with a minor ding in the fender and an empty gas tank, your dad happily reports the car's recovery to the police and to the insurance company.

The next week you drive to a friend's house. On the way home, you're pulled over by the police, told to get out of the car, pushed hard against the hood, and frisked. They inform you that you are driving a stolen car. Despite your protests and attempts to tell them what happened, you are handcuffed and taken to police headquarters.

Three hours later you're released, after your parents come to the station and records are checked with the motor vehicle administration. "Sorry," says the sergeant, "The computer has been down, and we didn't get the word that your car had been recovered."

Would you:

- Yell at the police as you left the station?
- Be glad the police were on the lookout for your family's car?
- Ask your family lawyer to sue the police department?
- Send a letter to city hall expressing outrage because you believe your rough treatment was based on your being a teen?
- Write down what happened as soon as you got home?

No matter which of the first four you picked, we hope you would also "write down what happened." Whenever you have any encounter with police, even a minor one, write down everything you remember as soon as you can. This includes events in which there was no arrest. Even being stopped by the police should be written down and recorded. Why?

- No one knows what will happen in the future.
- The police or someone else involved may decide to take the matter to court at a later date.
- If you have to go to court, you will need all the help you can get to present your side of the case clearly, logically, and truthfully. Documentation is always important to do this, and usually more accurate than your memory.

- If the situation involves someone else, you need a record of your views because the other person may not agree with the way you remember the event.
- You may later report the incident to the proper authorities.

The Written Report

Begin writing as soon as you can after the encounter, because time is crucial. When a lot of time passes, we all tend to forget a lot of facts and details. Since our brains are always working to make sense out of what happens to us, we add details because the story seems to make more sense that way.

Your report written at the time of an event will give a more accurate picture than the one in your mind months later. It will also add power to your spoken words if you report the officer or go to court. Any lawyer, judge, or jury in the United States will be impressed if a person appears with a written, dated report of what happened. You'll be showing maturity, and more weight will be given to your testimony, especially if it disagrees with the police report.

Police Records and Reports

As we noted before, police are required to keep records and file formal reports. These reports are a way for the department to keep track of what officers do. They show how often officers make arrests and what kinds of arrests they make. They also record circumstances surrounding incidents that happen on their shift.

The police report shows what the officer believes happened, based on talking with witnesses and people involved. Most of these records are as correct and truthful as the officer can make them—from the officer's point of view. What the officer reports may be correct, but it is still reported the way he or she saw it.

The report you write will obviously be from your point of view, and that is why you need it. Writing down what happened, however, is not simply a matter of making a few notes on scrap paper and tossing it in a drawer.

Mai didn't like to answer her apartment doorbell at night, but she could hear a young woman's voice pleading for help. Reluctantly, she opened the door, and a young woman rushed in. Her clothes were torn, her hair was flying.

"Please let me use your phone," she said, giving her name as Polly Miller. "My boyfriend tried to rape me. I jumped out of the car while it was moving, and I want my dad to come get me."

Her story sounded true, so Mai showed her the phone in the kitchen. The young woman made a tearful plea to her dad and was assured that he would be along shortly. She confirmed the address with Mai and told her dad to meet her outside in fifteen minutes.

While she waited, Polly asked if she might wash up. Mai showed her the bathroom and even got a fresh towel for her, but she cautiously stayed outside the bathroom door.

In a few minutes Polly came out and looked surprised to see Mai standing there. Hastily, she closed her backpack and mumbled that her dad would be waiting. She hurried out the door and down the stairs.

When Mai thought about it, she wondered why Polly had had her backpack open. Checking the bathroom medicine cabinet, she found that all of her prescription medicines were gone.

At once, she wrote a description of Polly, her clothes, how she talked, and what she said. She wrote down as much as she could remember of the phone conversation too. The next day she turned over her notes to the police. They were so accurate that the police were able to identify Polly as a well-known thief and to nab a gang that had been using that method to gain entrance to apartments. They stole not only drugs, but whatever they could from bedrooms as well. Mai received a thousand dollars in reward money.

The SNAP Record

Keeping records isn't hard. The way we'll show you is a SNAP. SNAP is a way of organizing and writing down what you have seen, heard, said, and done. If you ever report an officer or have to go to court, you'll be glad you have a SNAP report. Your life could depend on it.

In the back of this book is a blank SNAP report. Flip to it as you read what is needed in each part. Because an encounter with the police could be very different, you may need to add to the basic information we suggest.

Let's suppose your house was broken into when you were away. A neighbor, who promised to check your house, says all was well at four o'clock. But when you return at six, your television set, stereo system, and the money you kept in a bank on a shelf are all missing. You call the police.

As soon as the investigating officer leaves, use your computer, typewriter, or pen to write down the facts as you remember them.

The s in SNAP

The s in SNAP stands for State the facts first. A valuable report starts from the first moment of a police encounter, perhaps when you called for help, perhaps when the officer stopped you and asked you a question, or even the moment you thought you might be questioned by the police.

In this case, write the day, date, and time of the theft. Double-check to be sure you have the date right. For times you don't know, such as when the theft took place, give your best guess and say that the time is approximate. Any obviously incorrect information can make your SNAP report look as if your other facts are wrong too.

Don't forget to note the investigating officer's name and/or identification number. Most officers have their name on their uniform or their badge. If you can't get a name, get a number.

In the present theft case, you would write down where you were when the theft took place, what the neighbor did, what you did when you realized what had happened, and what the officer did when he or she checked out the theft. Report as fact only those things that you can see, smell, taste, touch or hear. Choose your words carefully.

Stating facts means never using "hot" words in writing your report. Keep your words cool. Cool words are those that state facts clearly and objectively.

Say something like this: "Mrs. Miles, my neighbor, had agreed to check on my house while I was away. She checked once, which she said was 'a few minutes after four PM,' and reports she did not see anything wrong at that time or hear anyone break in later."

You do not say: "The dumb jerk made just one quick check and then spent the rest of the time watching a TV show and wouldn't have heard the thief break in even if he had used dynamite."

"Dumb" and "jerk" are hot words, not facts. Hot words call people names, insult them, make fun of them, or suggest something you couldn't possibly know. (You can only guess that your neighbor made a "quick" check, unless she said so at the time. If she did not, you are only making a guess, not stating facts.) Hot words also make the person who reads your report later think you are making things up to get back at someone. A reader is more likely to believe you if your report sounds as fair as possible.

The N in SNAP

The N in SNAP stands for Name any others who were there. Describe them if you don't know their names. Perhaps while you were away a party was going on across the street. Someone there might have seen something that your neighbor didn't. Maybe they can back up what you say if you and your neighbor disagree later.

The A in SNAP

The A in SNAP stands for Add anything else. Add anything that will make clearer what happened. Again, use cool words to record your personal view of the incident. This is the place to record things like what you felt, whom you suspect, rumors, and so on. Read over your report. If you used a computer, print out a hard copy and make a backup disk. Computers automatically date a file, which also lends authenticity to your report.

Before you sign and date the finished report, we suggest that for any serious encounter you have your SNAP report notarized within seventy-two hours of the incident. Notaries are people appointed by the state. For a very small fee, the notary will watch you sign your name and date your report. Then the notary will also sign the report and imprint a seal on it. A notary can be found at banks and in many offices, such as real estate offices. Convenience stores often have a notary.

The signature and seal of a notary simply guarantee that you are the person who signed it. Having your report notarized doesn't mean that what you said is true, but it is proof that you signed your name as having written it and did so soon after the event. Again, this action on your part adds weight to your view of what happened and might sway a court to believe you.

If you do not have your SNAP report notarized, sign and date it yourself. Then make two copies of it. Send one copy to yourself in the mail. When you receive it, do *not* open it. The date on the envelope from the post office's cancellation of your stamp is a way of officially establishing the date of your report.

The P in SNAP

P stands for Put it away. Like all valuable records, a SNAP report should be kept in a safe place. Give the second copy to a responsible person you can count on, someone who will keep it as a backup in case you lose the original. If you have a safe deposit box, put the original there. If you are a minor, give the original to an adult to file away for you.

If you're not very good at writing, use a tape recorder. Or ask a friend or relative to write for you while you tell them what you want to say. Tell them not to change any words or correct the way you say it. You want to be able to swear that the report is yours and no one else's. No matter which format you use for recording the facts and information, check carefully by rereading or listening to the tape later to assure that each word is correct.

Auto Accidents: A Special Type of SNAP Report

If you are involved in an auto accident, especially as the driver of one of the cars, you will have to file a report covering details of the accident. You will need the facts for the police report and your insurance company. You may also need the report if you are sued by the other party in the accident.

The "Car Accident Information" form in the back of this book will help you assemble the facts you need to file a correct report. If an officer gives you a ticket or any other piece of paper, it should have the needed information on it, but don't rely only on using that.

Filing an Effective Complaint About the Police

First, be sure you want to make a complaint.

- Did you do anything to bring on the officer's behavior, such as cursing or not doing what you were asked? If you make a complaint just because you didn't like getting a ticket, you'll have a hard time persuading anyone to listen to you.
- If you make a complaint, realize that police may later go out of their way to catch you speeding or otherwise breaking the law. Unfortunately, that can

happen. We suggest you refer to Chapter 2 and
reflect on the immense power the police have.
- Can you handle having TV and news photographers
taking pictures of you and publishing the story? If
you make a good case against the police, that can
happen.

If you are underage or live at home, talk to your parents
first about filing a complaint, because what you do will
affect the whole family. Ask your family to help you list
and discuss the pros and cons of complaining. We aren't
trying to discourage you from filing a complaint but,
because the repercussions can be so great, we urge you
first to get advice from people you trust.

You may also want to contact members of community
organizations that advocate for private citizens and might
consider giving you support. Be clear that, at this point,
you are not sure what action you'll take.

If everyone agrees that further action is a good idea,
start by making a phone call to the chief of police or the
head of the civilian review board. Have your SNAP report
in front of you so that you can give the facts quickly. Be
patient. Don't expect action at once.

If nothing happens in a couple of weeks, make three
copies of your SNAP report. Always keep the original, no
matter who asks for it. Send the first copy to the chief of
police. If you don't get an answer in a few more weeks,
send a copy to the mayor or county executive or the governor—whoever is the police chief's boss.

If still nothing happens, send a copy with the whole
story to the editor of your newspaper or to the news editor
of the local TV station.

Again, be sure your complaint is worth the price you
may pay. If it is, go for it. That's how community change

takes place. Police who do wrong are punished by most police forces. They may not be treated as harshly as you would like, but something will usually be done.

Of course, justice is not always served. Not everyone, police or otherwise, who commits a crime is caught and punished.

But nothing happens if no one tries to change things for the better. You have a responsibility to obey the law. You also have a responsibility to see that others, including the police, obey the law too.

Police, Cops, the Man, the Law, the Feds, the Pigs, the Bluecoats, Bobbies, Brass Buttons, John Law, Fuzz

We have looked at the police from a number of points of view in this book. As we said at the beginning, the police are here to stay, and sooner or later you will encounter them. We hope you have gained information that will help you better deal with the police, for whatever reason you encounter them.

Glossary

Not all of these words appear in the text. However, they are words you may hear in connection with arrests and criminal proceedings.

accessory A person who helps with or knows about a crime before or after it is committed.

adjudicatory hearing The hearing of a juvenile case before a judge. Juvenile cases are rarely heard by juries.

alias A false name; a name used to deceive others about your true identity.

arraignment The hearing in which a defendant is informed of the charges and his/her rights and is asked to plead guilty or not guilty.

arrest The act of detaining someone for the purpose of charging him or her with breaking a law.

arrest warrant A paper issued by a judge ordering a law-enforcement officer to arrest a person who is believed to have broken the law.

bail Money paid to the court to guarantee that if you are allowed to go home you will show up in court when you are required.

beat The area a police officer patrols.

capital offense A crime that can be punished by death or life imprisonment.

case load The number of people that a social worker or parole officer must supervise.

cite (verb) To declare that the person committed an offense.

civilian review board   Group of citizens who watchdog the police department to be sure police are doing their duty properly.

crime   The act of breaking a law.

custody   Taking control of, or responsibility for, another person.

delinquency   A law violation that would be considered a crime if committed by an adult.

detention   Legally keeping a person in a holding facility of some kind.

DUI   Driving Under the Influence of drugs or alcohol.

DWI   Driving While Intoxicated.

felony   Serious crime, such as murder or rape.

frisk (verb)   To pat one's hands over the outer clothing of a suspect.

jail   Local facility for housing prisoners for a short time.

mandatory supervised release   *See* parole.

Miranda rights   The standard statement of rights that an officer must read to a suspect.

misdemeanor   A crime punishable by a year or less in jail.

murder   Willful and deliberate taking of a person's life.

parole   Release from prison before serving full time.

patrol   The area that an officer polices; similar to **beat**.

perpetrator   Person who commits a crime.

police brutality   Use of illegal physical force.

prison   Jail for long-term offenders.

probable cause   Good reason an officer has to think a crime has been, will be, or is being committed.

probation   Permission for a convicted criminal to go home instead of serving the time. If the criminal violates the conditions of probation, he or she then goes to prison.

reformatory   A prison for young offenders.

rookie   A first-year participant on the police force.

sentence   The penalty imposed on a criminal by the judge.

suspect   The person the police believe committed a crime.

take into custody   *See* arrest.

violation   Breaking of a very minor law, less than a misdemeanor; also called infraction.

warrant   Paper that directs an officer to do something, such as search a house to look for evidence of a crime.

Where to Go for Help

You will get the quickest and most personal help from a local authority, such as a school guidance counselor or a religious leader, or from groups, including local chapters of national organizations. Someone in your town or city is the best resource for direct advice or can tell you where to go to receive the information that will help with your specific problem or situation.

Here are some national resources to check for information:

American Civil Liberties Union (ACLU)
The national organization cannot process requests for assistance but suggests you check your local phone book for the number of the office near you.
Web site: http://www.aclu.org
This site will link you to the local ACLU chapter. You can also download a "bustcard," a quick guide to carry with you that briefly lists your rights and how to handle yourself in a police confrontation.

Center for Constitutional Rights
666 Broadway, 7th Floor
New York, NY 10012
(212) 614-6464
The Center for Constitutional Rights (CCR) is a nonprofit legal and educational corporation dedicated to advancing and protecting the rights guaranteed by the United States Constitution and the Universal Declaration of Human Rights. A pamphlet, "If an Agent Knocks: Federal Investigators and Your Rights" can be ordered from the address above or viewed online.

Web site: http://www.cs.oberlin.edu/students/pjaques/etext/ifanagentknocks.html

National Association for the Advancement of Colored People (NAACP)

The oldest and best-known group for minorities. Check your local telephone book or access its web site to find a chapter in your state.
Web site: http://local.naacp.org

Violence Against Women Office

A U.S. government office to help victims of violence and a source of information, including newsletters and press releases. For local referrals or confidential counseling, please call the National Domestic Violence Hot Line at (800) 799-SAFE or (800) 787-3224 (TTY). For emergencies, call your local police.
Web site: http://www.usdoj.gov/vawo

Other Web sites:

The Access to Justice Network (ACJNet) is a Canadian web site which offers help in both English and French.
Web site: http://www.acjnet.org

CopNet is a community service justice directory that will link you to hundreds of web sites in North and South America.
Web site: http://www.copnet.org

A world-wide law enforcement site that provides news and other related links.
Web site: http://www.ih2000.net/ira/ira.html

Police Guide offers over 1,700 fire and law enforcement listings around the world and access to the web pages of the Fraternal Order of Police and the International Police Association.
Web site: http://www.policeguide.com

Appendix

SNAP REPORT

_____ , _____ , _____ , _____

Day of week   Month   Date   Year

Investigated by:

Officer's name: _____

Badge #: _____ Incident #: _____

State/City/County/Dept: _____

State the facts

1. _____
_____
_____

2. _____
_____
_____

3. _____
_____
_____

4. _____
_____
_____

5. _____
_____
_____

Name others involved

Name: _____

Full address: _____

_____

Home phone: ____-____-____   Work phone: ____-____-____

Name: _____

Full address: _____

_____

Home phone: ____-____-____   Work phone: ____-____-____

Add other important information

_____

_____

_____

_____

_____

_____

_____

_____

_____
Signature

____/____/____   _____
Date   Name printed

Put this form in a safe place

Car Accident Information

My insurance company: _____

Policy #: _____

Agent's name & phone #: _____

Date/time of accident: ____/____/____, ____: ____ ____m.

Location (street names, route numbers, and other identifying information):

_____

_____

Other car in accident:

Make/model: _____ Year: _____

Driven by: _____

Full address: _____

Home phone: ____-____-____   Work phone: ____-____-____

Describe damage: _____

_____

Insurance company: _____

Policy #: _____

Investigated by:

Officer's name: _____ Badge #: _____

State/City/County/Dept: _____

Incident #: _____

Car Accident Information, page 2

Diagram of accident:

(Include street/road names, location of people, buildings, cars involved, etc.)

Car Accident Information, page 3

Witnesses (W) or Occupants (O) of cars:

Name: W/O   _____

Full address: _____

_____

Home phone: ____-____-____   Work phone: ____-____-____

Name: W/O   _____

Full address: _____

_____

Home phone: ____-____-____   Work phone: ____-____-____

Name: W/O   _____

Full address: _____

_____

Home phone: ____-____-____   Work phone: ____-____-____

Name: W/O   _____

Full address: _____

_____

Home phone: ____-____-____   Work phone: ____-____-____

Injured:

Name: W/O   _____

Full address: _____

_____

Home phone: ____-____-____   Work phone: ____-____-____

Type of injury: _____

Name: W/O   _____

Full address: _____

_____

Home phone: ____-____-____   Work phone: ____-____-____

Type of injury: _____

Car Accident Information, page 4

Other damage caused by accident:

Damage was to the following property: _____
Describe the damage:

_____
_____
_____
_____

Other important information:

_____
_____
_____
_____
_____

For Further Reading

Atkinson, L. *Your Legal Rights*. New York: Franklin Watts, 1982.

Bornstein, J. *Police Brutality: A National Debate*. Hillside, NJ: Enslow Publishers, Inc., 1993.

Cohen, P. and S. *Careers in Law Enforcement and Security*. New York: The Rosen Publishing Group, 1995.

Dautrich, J. and V. Huff. *Big City Detective*. New York: Lodestar Books, 1986.

Gardner, R. *Crime Lab 101*. New York: Walker and Co., 1992.

Hewett, J. *Public Defender: Lawyer for the People*. New York: Lodestar Books, 1991.

Humes, E. *No Matter How Loud I Shout: A Year in the Life of Juvenile Court*. New York: Simon & Schuster, 1996.

Hyde, M.O. *Kids In and Out of Trouble: Juveniles and the Law*. New York: Cobblehill, 1995.

Inciardi, J.A. *Criminal Justice*. New York: Harcourt, Brace Jovanovich, Publishers, 1990.

Loeb, R.H., Jr. *Crime and Capital Punishment*. New York: Franklin Watts, 1986.

Routier, W.J., M.C. Larkin and B. Chorak. *Law in Your Life*. Minneapolis: West Publishing Company (in press).

Seuling, B. *It is Illegal to Quack Like a Duck*. New York: Lodestar Books, 1988.

Wirths, Claudine G. *Choosing a Career in Law Enforcement*. New York: The Rosen Publishing Group, 1997.

Index